Jim White has had a lifelong interest in wildlife and an active concern for nature conservation. He grew up in south Hampshire in what was then still rural countryside with relatively easy access to a variety of interesting habitats, giving him a good all round grounding in natural history. After graduating from London University with a first class honours degree in Botany, he started research based at the Field Centre at Slapton Ley on the south Devon coast. But only a year on, the opportunity to take his first full-time job managing the 460 acre nature reserve at Slapton was too good to miss! After a further three years, he moved back to Hampshire to become the first professional Conservation Officer of the Hampshire and Isle of Wight Wildlife Trust. This was followed by 18 months as Ecologist with Hampshire County Council and then the move to Dorset in 1979 to work for the Nature Conservancy Council. NCC became English Nature in 1991 and soon after Jim's job changed, from Assistant Regional Officer to Dorset Team Manager. Though his work is now largely centred around the office Jim still has a passionate interest in all aspects of nature conservation and he considers himself very fortunate to have been able to combine his great personal interest with his profession.

Following page
Two 'classic' blue butterflies of chalk and limestone turf –
the widespread common blue and the much more local,
powder blue chalkhill.

DISCOVER DORSET

DOWNS, MEADOWS & PASTURES

JIM WHITE

THE DOVECOTE PRESS

This book is dedicated to the memory of my late mother, who loved wild flowers and who generously indulged my passion for nature in opportunities she never had.

Horseshoe vetch in flower on the Bronze Age earthworks at Knowlton, one of Dorset's ancient fragments of downland.

First published in 2003 by The Dovecote Press Ltd
Stanbridge, Wimborne, Dorset BH21 4JD

ISBN 1 904349 08 0

© Jim White 2003

Jim White has asserted his rights under the Copyright, Designs and Patent Act 1988 to be identified as author of this work

Series designed by Humphrey Stone

Typeset in Monotype Sabon
Printed and bound in Singapore

A CIP catalogue record for this book is available
from the British Library

1 3 5 7 9 8 6 4 2

CONTENTS

A BYGONE AGE

Of all the habitats now valued for nature conservation there is probably none more evocative of a bygone age – a time of plenty for wildlife – than grasslands. True that marvellous old woods and rare expanses of heath are also windows into the past, but maybe it is because grassland of one form or another is still abundant, albeit of minimal nature conservation value, that we can so readily see the scale of what has gone.

The tiny fragments of grassland still rich in herbs and grasses, whether on limestone or acid, neutral, wet or dry soils, are but a minute proportion of what once existed, even in a county like Dorset. The losses are quite recent. Many of us can recall, increasingly distantly, childhood memories of flowery meadows, turned to sweet-smelling hay stacks in high summer; or aromatic, springy downland turf humming with insects, and fascinating damp hollows sparkling with kingcups and milkmaids in spring. We can still go to places, treasured sites perhaps in favourite nature reserves, where all of these are still to be found. But our annual pilgrimages to see the cowslips or the blue butterflies probably mean passing mile upon mile of re-seeded blue-green leys or permanent pastures burgeoning with grass responding to fertiliser, to the exclusion of most flowers. Until quite recently many of these fields would have held the same turf that we now have to travel miles to see.

It is only since the massive and cheap availability of inorganic fertilisers and the armoury of chemicals to eradicate weeds and pests that the major changes to grasslands have happened. Before the Second World War, grasslands would have, of course, been ploughed, but reversion occurred quite readily, without the chemical applications

Opposite page A patch of herb-rich grassland following the clays near Beaminster.

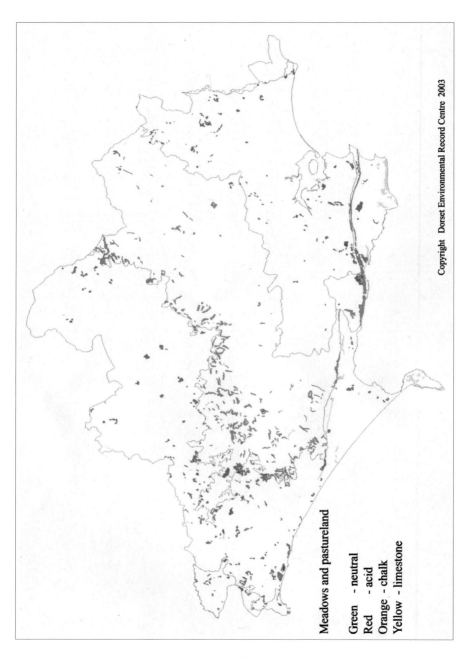

Meadows and pastureland

Green - neutral
Red   - acid
Orange - chalk
Yellow - limestone

Copyright Dorset Environmental Record Centre 2003

Clear traces of earlier cultivation with a pattern of 'Celtic' fields on steep slopes near Sydling, now growing fine chalk turf.

of today. Many old grasslands, too difficult or poor to plough, would have been traditionally cut for hay or grazed, producing less of a crop and maintaining fewer livestock. Only in the last 50 years has the declining quality of our grasslands become so evident and, perhaps worse, so irreversible.

Much is rightly made of ancient habitats. What has taken centuries, even millenia to evolve, cannot be replaced with ease once lost. We should think of such sites – an ancient forest with veteran trees or the wind-blown turf of an Iron Age hillfort – with no less awe and wonder than we routinely feel for more recent, man-made treasures such as medieval cathedrals or great works of art. With grasslands of nature

Opposite page The highly fragmented nature of surviving grasslands of wildlife interest is made clear by the map. Though widely spread across Dorset, these grasslands closely reflect geology and topography, with most of the chalk downland along the northern and western scarp of the chalk outcrop, the steeper slopes of the heads of the valleys and along the southern ridgeway and Purbeck hills. Limestone turf is very restricted, mainly in the south of the Isle of Purbeck and on Portland. Neutral pastures are most widely scattered but with a concentration in the clay vales of Marshwood and to a lesser extent Blackmore; while acid grassland, the scarcest grassland type, is restricted to the fringes of the heaths and hilltops in the far west.

conservation value, age is not the only important factor, however. Such sites can have high interest even if the turf may have been broken in the past. The hillforts, celtic fields, strip lynchets, trackways and more recent cultivations have often reverted to grasslands of outstanding nature conservation importance today. The critical factor is whether the soils have been modified and the nutrient status increased.

Compared with heathlands on free-draining sandy soils, grasslands have usually developed over more water retentive soils with at least some clay fraction. Nutrients like phosphates bind readily to the clay particles and do not easily leach from the soil. A fertiliser application can thus substantially alter the balance of the soil chemistry; the higher nutrient level favours the few demanding species, like certain grasses, that dominate and crowd out the original mix of perhaps 30 or 40 wild grasses and herbs. Repeated a few times and backed up with weedkillers, the original vegetation is effectively lost. Such has been the fate of most of our herb-rich grasslands. In 1984 the then Nature Conservancy Council estimated that 95% of all grassland in Great Britain had lost its nature conservation value. Much of that loss will have happened in the past 50 years.

Grassland would once have been naturally rare. In the time of the wild-wood, before our Stone Age ancestors started to make an impact

Impressive medieval lynchets – banks between cultivated strips – on the limestone downs in Purbeck.

Looking north from the chalk downs near Minterne across the claylands of the Blackmore Vale in early spring. Despite the appearance of a green landscape little grassland of wildlife interest still remains.

and began the forest clearance to farm stock and crops, what we now take for granted as the classic English patchwork of fields, had not emerged. But the latest thinking on the wildwood suggests that it was not a uniformly dense, heavily wooded landscape. Rather there will have been natural clearings caused by tree fall or wind-blow, maintained for a while by the large numbers of wild and later domestic herbivores, before natural tree regeneration filled the gaps – thus completing the cycle. Also at the extremes of exposure on the loftiest, bleakest sites, or strongly influenced by the sea, there may always have been open habitat suitable for grassland species.

In Dorset it is perhaps easiest to envisage this on newly formed features such as sand or shingle beaches and river or sea cliffs kept free from trees through natural erosion. The periodic landslips that have formed the great undercliffs of our county, such as at White Nothe,

Worbarrow Bay, Golden Cap and Lyme will have swept away woody species every so often and provided open conditions where today's grassland plants and animals could maintain a toehold. Then as the increasing effects of tree clearance, cultivation and grazing of both wild and domestic stock had their effect, the wonderful range of grasslands started to evolve. Over many centuries, in response to different soils and under a continuous pattern of use – of grazing or regular cutting or deliberate flooding – our grasslands developed.

Like heathland, grassland is often called man-made, but this is to credit humans with a skill and an intention beyond their ability. Bronze Age man did not set out with a vision of the heathland landscape as his goal, nor did the stone and iron-tooled tribes of the chalk hills mix wildflower and grass seed to create meadow or downland turf. The grassland we see today, where it has not been transformed by modem agriculture, is the result of nature's response to centuries of a constant management influence – grazing or cutting – on the particular local conditions of soil and climate. Thus, on the chalk uplands, from Eggardon Hill in the south-west, across our county and as far away as the Yorkshire Wolds, downland turf of a broadly similar character evolved. On the heavier, more fertile clay soils of every English county, pastures of a similar floral composition have developed.

No-one planted the wild thyme and clustered bellflowers; the green-winged orchids and spring sedge; the quaking grass or meadow oat. These and many other herbs, grasses and sedges are the constant components of different grassland sites on comparable soils with the same long history of management influence, the length and breadth of the country. To add to a fascinating constancy that would defeat even the most sophisticated modern habitat re-creation project, there is the subtle variation we find across the range of sites. So in the drier, hotter south-east, the chalk is classically orchid-rich. At its western limit in Dorset where rainfall is significantly more, there are naturally fewer orchids but the abundance of devil's-bit scabious (*Succisa pratensis*), betony (*Betonica officinalis*) and rough hawkbit (*Leontodon hispidus*) are striking character features. More locally still such differences are apparent. On the chalk of north-east Dorset, extending to our neighbouring counties of north-west Hampshire and south Wiltshire,

Cattle grazing amidst the cowslips on the Iron Age hillfort of Hod Hill.

the nationally scarce dwarf sedge (*Carex humilis*) is locally abundant on suitable sites, but nowhere else, even though apparently suitable chalk grassland sites still occur to the east and west.

These are puzzles, perhaps to solve and certainly to marvel at. They take the richness and fascination of this plant community far beyond the dry inquiry – what orchids does it have? Indeed because herb-rich grassland was abundant not so long ago in every county, the number of really rare species is limited. Even rapidly declining species like green-winged orchid (*Orchis morio*) were widespread if local. This has made a realisation of the plight of surviving rich grassland and its defence even more difficult.

TYPES OF GRASSLAND

CHALK GRASSLAND

Though grassland worthy of conservation is today very limited, both in Dorset and nationally, there are various types with different characteristic species. Most plentiful in Dorset is grassland that has developed over chalk and limestone soils. The great swathe of chalk country that strikes a diagonal band south-west to north-east across the county, with a narrow tail across the south, forms the familiar Dorset Downs and Purbeck Hills. It carries on north, through Cranborne Chase, into Hampshire and Wiltshire, splitting into the North and South Downs and the Chilterns, all with their fragments of surviving chalk downland. The narrow southern limb forms the spine of the Isle of Wight, whose chalk cliffs of Tennyson Down and the Needles can be glimpsed from Ballard Cliff and Old Harry rocks, their immediate counterpart in our county.

From the concentration of ancient earthworks on the chalk downs we can suppose that this landscape was amongst the first to emerge extensively as the original forest of the wildwood was cleared. Perhaps the commanding positions and possibly the thinner more easily worked soil and correspondingly less vigorous trees made the downland heights especially attractive to our early forebears. We are left today with the still awe-inspiring remains of their settlements; but the scale of clearance to make the hillforts and camps must have extended well beyond their present bounds. The ramparts that we see today would have been revetted with timber, consuming thousands of trees, probably from managed woodland such as coppice.

Stand on the heights of Hambledon Hill, and imagine its tiered banks lined with paling, and the scale of the work and its impact on the surrounding land starts to emerge. Originally such ramparts were bare, gleaming chalk, but in the millenia that have passed, turf has developed over the banks. It is often these steep, drained, thin-soiled

The spring combination of cowslips and early purple orchids on the slopes of Hambledon Hill National Nature Reserve.

The still impressive earthworks of Badbury Rings, created over 2000 years ago and today carrying flower-rich turf.

banks that support the best surviving herb-rich turf.

There is evidence that some chalk plants only occur on this most ancient of turf, in existence for perhaps 3000 years or more and never ploughed. Such rarities in Dorset include burnt orchid (*Orchis ustulata*), hovering on the eastern county boundary, on the massive Bokerly Dyke, and field fleawort (*Tephroseris integrifolia*) on earthworks, as on Hod Hill. Some plants though, despite a reputation for lack of colonising ability, clearly can move into more recent grassland. Bee orchid (*Ophrys apifera*) for instance is not uncommon in the turf that has grown over old quarries, or even shell holes in the Army Ranges. Even early spider-orchid (*Ophrys sphegodes*), though usually a component of old turf, can flourish in the more recent grassland of abandoned quarries. Yet other chalk herbs occur only where the turf has been disturbed and so are not regular components of the ancient turf. Such early colonists include kidney vetch (*Anthyllis vulneraria*) and the two frequent umbellifers of chalky soils, wild carrot (*Daucus carota*) and wild parsnip (*Pastinaca sativa*).

The theme of rich turf surviving only on steep ground is repeated away from the hillfort earthworks. In general only the steepest natural downland slopes still carry flowery grassland. The ancient sheepwalks that stretched across countless thousands of acres of the southern chalk have long since gone to the plough and much now grows cereals.

Two orchids with different needs. Bee orchid (*left*) is not infrequent and can establish in quite recent grassland like abandoned quarries. Burnt orchid (*right*) seems to need ancient turf and only occurs in Dorset on the great earthwork marking our eastern boundary.

Ancient downland being ploughed in 1942 on easy slopes near Winterborne Kingston. Today this area only supports arable fields or re-seeded leys.

The pattern is easily seen in Dorset on the gentle slopes of the broad dip slope of the chalk, rising gradually from the heathland basin. Almost no chalk grassland survives here. It is not until there is a valley with steeper sides cutting into this landscape, or the scarp slope plunges away to the vales around the outer edges of the chalk massif, that the more substantial chalk grassland fragments appear.

The local concentrations of good chalk grassland, rich in flowers and often insects too, tend then to follow the outer, higher and steeper margins of the chalk. The Purbeck Ridge, which reaches the coast in spectacular switchback plunges between Flowers Barrow and White Nothe, is one such spot. Some of the valley sides of rivers like the Cerne and Sydling and other tributaries of the Frome and Stour provide surviving slopes. The scarp slope itself, especially at its extremities, as at Melbury Down in the north and Eggardon and Haydon in the west, is another area where chalk grassland has survived.

Very little unimproved grassland remains on the flatter chalk since almost always this has been available for cultivation. Only where this has been prevented for some reason do we get a hint of such a landscape. Part of Bindon Range behind Lulworth still has gently rolling chalk grassland, like a little piece of Salisbury Plain transposed; and the western end of the Purbeck Ridge top, between Whiteway Hill and Flowers Barrow, and the top of Bindon Hill itself, have rare examples of hilltop turf. Elsewhere such flat surfaces have been ploughed and even where they have been put back to grassland, the turf has little of its original character. It is interesting but perhaps not surprising that these examples are all within Ministry of Defence land, where agricultural progress has been largely frozen since the 1940s.

The chalk outcrop is the most obvious area of calcareous soils, and thus it is here that most chalk grassland survives in Dorset. But there are other areas with calcareous rock and these also can support fine, herb-rich turf. The most concentrated and well-known of the limestone areas in Dorset is in the extreme south, forming the Isle of Portland and part of the Purbeck coast, between Swanage and St Aldhelm's Head. Here the Purbeck and Portland limestones form not only the spectacular cliff coast but underlie much of the nearby land. Wherever this survives as grassland, and especially in the long sweep

Rich turf on the floor of an abandoned limestone quarry
at Kingbarrow, Portland.

from Durlston to Worth Matravers, 'chalk' grassland can be found, but it is not all ancient. The clear and striking marks of earlier cultivations are evident near Worth and Seacombe with wonderful tiers of medieval lynchet banks, and more recent quarries here and on Portland have regrown some excellent herb-rich turf. The common factors are thin, lime-rich soils, unaffected by fertilisers. Many of the components of grassland on the chalk are present here on the limestone, but there are some differences too.

There are outcrops of limestone elsewhere in Dorset, but less extensively. Little fragments of 'chalk' turf can sometimes be found, indicating limestone soils, where agricultural improvement has not completely altered the grassland. The narrow limestone band north of Weymouth has such examples, as does the odd larger site – like Chalbury Hill. Further inland pockets of the Inferior Oolite can be traced with revealing turf, as near Powerstock Castle and around Sherborne.

Whilst there is a strong common thread running through all calcareous grassland, with many species present throughout, there are also differences. Perhaps because the limestones are often harder, but also because they are often covered by a deeper clay-rich soil than much of the chalk, the calcareous influence can be less marked. The turf over the Dorset limestones, especially those outcrops away from the coast, has some similarities with neutral grassland and perhaps only the more obvious chalk indicator plants are frequent. Wherever herbs like salad burnet (*Sanguisorba minor*), hoary plantain (*Plantago media*) and stemless thistle (*Cirsium acaule*) occur there is some calcareous influence. On dry grassland sites the presence of glaucous sedge (*Carex flacca*), quaking grass (*Briza media*), wild thyme (*Thymus polytrichus*) and common bird's-foot-trefoil (*Lotus corniculatus*) can be expected and though not confined to chalk and limestone, they are frequent here. Then there is a long list of more exacting chalk herbs and mosses, scarcely found away from these soils. Such gems as small scabious (*Scabiosa columbaria*), horseshoe vetch (*Hippocrepis comosa*), common rock-rose (*Helianthemum nummularium*) and clustered bellflower (*Campanula glomerata*) are typical of this select group, along with a number of rarer species, found perhaps only on a handful of sites.

We all have our favourite downland flowers, perhaps evoking a memory of a site from early botanising days; seeing such plants is like meeting old friends again. Many of us will be content to note these individual species; others may go further and make a list of all plants present, including the grasses and mosses. If this is done on a range of sites it may be possible to notice that there are several fairly distinct plant communities, even within the category of chalk grassland.

The most widespread of these associations, representing classic chalk and limestone grassland, is herb-rich turf with many species of fine-leaved grasses and rosette-forming herbs, in which no single species dominates. Indeed this is the famous turf in which it is not uncommon to find upwards of 25 different species within a single metre square. Some of those plants listed above will be joined by squinancywort (*Asperula cynanchica*), sheep's fescue (*Festuca ovina*), meadow oat-grass (*Helictotrichon pratensis*), lady's bedstraw (*Galium verum*), burnet-saxifrage (*Pimpinella saxifraga*) and autumn gentian

Opposite page The top photographs are of two 'faithful' and widespread indicators of chalk and limestone – salad burnet (*left*) and hoary plantain. The lower photographs are of more exacting and less frequent chalk herbs – rockrose (*left*) and clustered bellflower.

Left Autumn gentian or felwort – one of the latest of the summer chalk flowers.
Right Vibrant blue chalk milkwort flowers on a few downlands in late spring.

Gentianella amarella, with added spice provided by less widespread plants like early gentian (*G. anglica*), hairy rock-cress (*Arabis hirsuta*), chalk milkwort *Polygala calcarea* and, if you look really carefully, bastard-toadflax (*Thesium humifusum*).

This classic chalk turf has a variant that is particularly well shown in Dorset, and which is especially conspicuous in late summer when the blue and purple of many of the flowers creates a distinctive and attractive haze over the downland. Most of the regular flowers and grasses are there, but devil's-bit and small scabious, betony, saw-wort (*Serratula tinctoria*), clustered bellflower and ox-eye daisy (*Leucanthemum vulgare*) are notably frequent. The strikingly western distribution of this grouping on the English chalk and limestone is perhaps a reflection of the wetter conditions, especially in winter, together with the warm summer conditions typical of southern localities. The higher incidence of traditional cattle grazing on the downs in Dorset may also be significant in the evolution of this beautiful grassland.

Within these variations of classic chalk turf, plants and their dependant insects show their locational preferences. The typical devil's-bit/betony turf is especially linked to west and south-west

Cowslips and early purple orchid on a downland slope.

facing slopes. Horseshoe-vetch and perhaps rockrose, however, are most often found on south facing slopes. The north and east facing downs may have fewer herbs, though cowslip (*Primula veris*) and pignut (*Conopodium majus*) are often more plentiful and the turf is often richer in mosses, less prone to drying out on these moister slopes. The seasons bring their changes too. In early summer it is the time of vetches, and splashes of bright yellow bird's-foot-trefoil and horseshoe vetch contrast with the blue and pink of milkworts. The unusual combination of cowslips and early-purple orchids (*Orchis mascula*) is another attractive local feature of some of our downs.

Early spider orchid has its best colonies in Dorset, but only on the limestone slopes of Purbeck.

Another fairly distinctive association of chalk and limestone flora, again very typical of western Britain is that of short, tussocky turf with sheep's-fescue the main grass, found around outcrops of the hardest chalk and limestone rock. This community can be found where rock breaks through the normal turf, on bluffs and clifftops: in Dorset the coastal limestone and hard chalk of the Purbeck Ridge are its home. Other characteristic plants are carline thistle (*Carlina vulgaris*), wild thyme, mouse-ear-hawkweed (*Pilosella officinarum*) and yellow-wort (*Blackstonia perfoliata*), with occasionally the rare early gentian in early summer, as along the sparse clifftop vegetation of Ballard Cliff.

The coastal chalk and limestone are also the main home in Dorset of another plant community in which the coarse tor-grass (*Brachypodium pinnatum*) is dominant. Much maligned and even feared by chalk grassland managers, tor-grass turf is, in fact, of very restricted distribution in Britain. Its bad reputation stems from the rank nature of the turf when ungrazed, often to the exclusion of most

The Dorset Wildlife Trust nature reserve at Townsend, near Swanage has rich turf over former limestone quarries and spoil banks. Horses keep this turf well grazed.

typical chalk herbs. When well managed, however, tor-grass turf can be almost as rich as classic chalk grassland, though there are plenty of examples of its less appealing form. The limestone of Purbeck and the sweep of chalk across the south of Dorset are its main locations, though small patches prosper on a few inland sites.

Ungrazed, this turf has few component species able to compete with the tall, coarse grass. Glaucous sedge, stinking iris (*Iris foetidissima*) and wood-sage (*Teucrium scorodonia*) can persist under such conditions, but when the turf is properly grazed there are plenty of attractive herbs and grasses. Perhaps foremost among these is the early spider orchid, in Dorset only found in tor-grass turf on Purbeck's limestone. One of the localities for this intriguing plant, indeed its only spot away from the coastal slope, is Townsend Nature Reserve near Swanage. In the early 1980s this was a mass of deep tor-grass, with only the steep banks and mounds of the former quarry still carrying short, open turf. The prospect of trying to control tor-grass by cutting

Meadow saxifrage, nodding in a late spring breeze, grows in the deeper soil between the great Iron Age ramparts of Hambledon Hill.

and removing material seemed impossibly daunting for the Dorset Wildlife Trust. Then the opportunity to graze with a couple of horses came along, transforming the site. This exercise in the value of horse grazing as an aid to management was used later by the National Trust on its Spyway and Seacombe property in Purbeck, where Exmoor ponies have brought the extensive limestone grassland back into good condition after a spell attempting to rely on sheep. So for tor-grass turf, grazing by older horses or cattle is the answer; sheep are useless! Where a thatch of old grass has developed an initial burn may help so long as this is small in scale and is followed by appropriate grazing.

In its most extreme coastal localities tor-grass turf can retain its diversity even without grazing. Perhaps exposure to wind, salt and sun is influential, with the added bonus of the thatch of dead leaves so typical of ungrazed sites being blown away from these coastal slopes. This taller but still diverse turf can be seen between White Nothe and Bat's Head, and again on the descent from Gad Cliff to Worbarrow Bay. Saw-wort seems to be particularly prominent in the sward in such places and pyramidal orchid (*Anacamptis pyramidalis*) is also quite frequent.

A further restricted grassland type occurs on our calcareous soils, again with a coarse grass dominating. Upright brome (*Bromopsis erecta*) is the key species, and this is rather like tor-grass in its unpalatable qualities. There are only small areas of this turf in Dorset – on the Isle of Portland, scattered across Purbeck, and in some spots on the northern inland chalk.

Within many of the chalk and limestone sites there are often pockets of grassland of slightly different character, in which yet another range of plants can grow. In the bottom of dry valleys, at the foot of the steep downs and also in the hollows between ancient earthworks, a deeper soil has usually accumulated, encouraging a wider range of plants to appear. One of the most noticeable is the delicate meadow saxifrage (*Saxifraga granulata*) that adorns parts of the hilltop at Hambledon.

Anthills are a feature of many old grassland sites free from recent ploughing, including downland. Again, due to the industry of their builders, yellow meadow ants (*Lasius flavus*), these hummocks present sifted, free-draining soils with somewhat different properties from the surrounding grassland. More diminutive plants can often grow here amongst the fine grass, and these may include concentrations of mouse-ear-hawkweed, wild thyme and early whitlow grass (*Erophila verna*). An attractive local moss (*Rhodobryum roseum*) occurs only in this habitat on a few downland sites.

NEUTRAL GRASSLAND

There is no absolute cut-off point between the different grassland types. Elements of the flora of chalk or limestone soils will continue into pastures over other rock types that have a calcareous influence. Thus clay soils on the Fuller's Earth, Forest Marble and some of the other Dorset Jurassic rocks can support neutral grassland in which a few familiar chalk plants still occur. At the other end of the spectrum there is a gradation from acid grassland into full-scale heathland or mire, seen most clearly perhaps over the Greensand soils and on some sites on the Tertiary clays around the margins of the heathland basin in south-east Dorset. But in its typical form neutral grassland is distinctive, attractive – and sadly now scarce.

Only some 1400 hectares of herb-rich neutral grassland remains in Dorset today and much of this is in small fragments, even single fields

A flower-rich hay field at the Wildlife Trust's Kincombe nature reserve.
Such meadows would have been common on damp neutral soils across
Dorset until quite recently.

or parts of fields. Nonetheless it is widely, if very thinly, scattered, since until perhaps 50 years ago such grassland was common in most parishes, wherever clay soils occur. Fine sites are still left then across the county, from a cluster of small fields near Shaftesbury in the north to a few pockets along the coast in the south; from Wootton and Lyme in the west across to the Avon valley in the east. Such fields of neutral grassland will be managed as permanent pasture, typically with cattle grazing, and in some cases as traditional hay fields with or without grazing in late summer, after the hay cut. The particular management, as well as the soil type and its wetness will affect the components of the turf and no two sites are the same, but there is a consistent character.

A range of grasses forms the turf, with no single species dominating. Typically perennial rye-grass (*Lolium perenne*), the ubiquitous component of agriculturally improved grassland, is present at only low level. Crested dog's-tail (*Cynosurus cristatus*), red fescue (*Festuca rubra*), Yorkshire-fog (*Holcus lanatus*), common bent (*Agrostis capillaris*) and sweet-vernal grass (*Anthoxanthum odoratum*) are all frequent, and in some sites quaking grass, heath-grass (*Danthonia decumbens*) and the attractive meadow barley (*Hordeum secalinum*) may also occur. Sedges are much more varied and frequent than on the chalk, with glaucous sedge, spring-sedge (*Carex caryophyllea*), carnation sedge (*C. panicea*), oval sedge (*C. ovalis*) and hairy sedge (*C. hirta*) all common, perhaps joined on a few rich sites, at the wetter end of the range, by flea sedge (*C. pulicaris*) and tawny sedge (*C. hostiana*).

Many herbs occur in the best examples of neutral grassland, creating an attractive and colourful sward. Common knapweed (*Centaurea nigra*), ox-eye daisy, clovers, dandelion (*Taraxacum officinale*), meadow vetchling (*Lathyrus pratensis*) and buttercups are bold and obvious components but a large number of other herbs can occur, some of them much less common. Lady's bedstraw, yarrow (*Achillea millifolium*) and agrimony (*Agrimonia eupatoria*) are most frequent in those pastures with a more calcareous influence, whilst the attractive mix of devil's-bit, betony, tormentil (*Potentilla erecta*) and pignut probably reflects a slightly more acidic tendency.

In the best sites there will be one or more of several much less

Two rather inconspicuous and local plants of high quality neutral grasslands – adder's-tongue fern (*left*) and pepper-saxifrage.

frequent plants, such as lady's-mantle (*Alchemilla vulgaris*), adder's-tongue fern (*Ophioglossum vulgatum*), pepper-saxifrage (*Silaum silaus*), dyer's greenweed (*Genista tinctoria*) and that Dorset speciality, corky-fruited water-dropwort (*Oenanthe pimpinelloides*) – a herb only found in this country in central southern England, with Dorset the centre of its distribution. It appears to survive some agricultural improvement so can sometimes persist in otherwise uninteresting

Neutral grasslands in Dorset are the best locality for the impossibly named corky-fruited water-dropwort.

Meadows like the Dorset Wildlife Trust nature reserve at Corfe Mullen, with masses of green-winged orchids are now very scarce.

grassland, but is a regular component of the best of Dorset's surviving meadows and pastures.

Also typical of the best neutral grasslands, though sadly scarce in Dorset, is green-winged orchid. There are now few fields with this quietly handsome flower in profusion, but the Dorset Wildlife Trust's nature reserve at Corfe Mullen has saved one such traditional meadow.

Wild daffodils still occur in a few grasslands over clay,
as here at Wootton Fitzpaine.

At the opposite end of the county, at Wootton Fitzpaine, there is a small group of fine fields where wild daffodils (*Narcissus pseudonarcissus*) still flower, to be followed by a scattering of green-winged orchids throughout the herb-rich turf.

Most of the plants will occur whether the grass is grazed or cut for hay. Yellow-rattle (*Rhinanthus minor*) is more fussy. As an annual, the distribution of its early ripening seeds is much helped by hay-making. Its semi-parasitic habit can under some circumstances locally weaken the vigour of the grasses in the sward, thus reducing the hay crop. Grazing hinders the distribution of its seed, so a season of grazing rather than hay-making is usually enough to restore the balance.

While the sward may be of fairly even composition throughout these few precious neutral grassland meadows and pastures, damper features can add to the diversity. This is most obvious where springs emerge or cause water to approach the surface in flushes, often where the underlying geology changes. An examination of the older, 2½" O.S. maps will reveal a fairly widespread use of marsh symbols, but often as not a field visit now will show little trace of the feature they once symbolised, or the additional species they encouraged. Not many have survived drainage and reclamation but where they have, they are exciting sites indeed.

A transition from relatively free-draining soils to more impeded drainage may give rise to springs or flushes. A classic occurrence of this is where the Greensand is underlain by heavier clays. Some of the small fields between Morcombelake and the coast, and the Toller/Kingcombe area, show this feature well. At Kingcombe the valley of the River Hooke cuts through the slightly base-rich Fuller's Earth and this underlies the bottom of the saucer. The higher, outer edges of the vale are formed by Greensand, over a narrow band of impervious Gault Clay. This feature occurs on the north and south sides of the valley, but on the north side the Greensand itself is overlain by Chalk, a variation reflected in the character of the grassland and the flushes that occur.

Walking south from the Dorset Wildlife Trust nature reserve base at Pound Cottage, Kingcombe, the first few fields are rich neutral grassland, with such gems as lady's mantle and corky-fruited water dropwort amongst the many other flowers. The flush line is encountered at about mid-slope and has small mires that have a different vegetation from the fields. Purple moor-grass (*Molinia caerulea*), bent grasses and Sphagnum mosses dominate the wettest areas, often with abundant marsh violet (*Viola palustris*), here the food plant of the increasingly scarce small pearl-bordered fritillary butterfly (*Boloria selene*). Marsh pennywort (*Hydrocotyle vulgaris*),

The scattered colonies of small pearl-bordered fritillary butterflies in acid flushes depend on marsh violets.

An acid flush at Kingcombe with a fine display of heath spotted-orchids.

meadow thistle (*Cirsium dissectum*), lousewort (*Pedicularis sylvatica*), heath spotted-orchid (*Dactylorhiza maculata*) and petty whin (*Genista anglica*), uncommon in Dorset, occur in the damp sward around these flushes and the rushes here are soft rush (*Juncus effusus*) and jointed rush (*J. articulatus*). All of these indicate acidic conditions, and this is further confirmed by the local occurrence of cross-leaved heath (*Erica tetralix*).

A similar walk north from Pound Cottage will lead to Mary Well and the flushed field above Mary Well Withy Bed. There is little sign here of any of the flush vegetation of the south side of the valley. Instead the wet turf has hard rush (*J. inflexus*), meadowsweet (*Filipendula ulmaria*), ragged robin (*Lychnis flos-cuculi*), great horsetail (*Equisetum telmateia*) and the occasional common-spotted (*Dactylorhiza fuchsii*) or marsh orchid (*D. praetermissa*). On this side of the valley, water drains through a capping of chalk as well as greensand, before meeting the clay; on the south side rain falls directly onto the greensand soils and unlike the chalk, these are acidic. With the wet features in neutral grassland then, their character is often more influenced by overlying than underlying geology.

The flushes and especially the base-rich fens that still survive around the edges of the chalk outcrop in west Dorset are rich not only for their plants; a handful of such sites support a diverse community

Marsh fritillary butterfly has declined drastically in its traditional wet grassland sites but there are a few strong colonies on the western chalk downs with their abundant devil's-bit scabious.

of invertebrates including several nationally scarce species. Craneflies, snail-killing flies, soldier flies, leaf beetles, soldier beetles and weevils are among the scarce insects, and spiders and snails also contribute to the rich mix of largely unnoticed wildlife in these fascinating and usually small-scale habitats of grassland and fen.

Damp rather than very wet pastures with an abundance of devil's-bit are the traditional habitat of one of our most rapidly declining butterflies, the marsh fritillary (*Eurodryas aurinia*). This still thrives in a few such marshy fields in Dorset, including a colony in a superb fragment of surviving old grass and fen in the Blackmore Vale. Rather oddly, marsh fritillary is also found on a few of the Dorset chalk downland sites where its foodplant is common and the turf is grazed appropriately by cattle. So scarce is marsh fritillary, that the wet grassland area and the cluster of chalk grasslands are now sites of European importance for this species.

There is often a gradation of neutral grassland into wetter fen conditions. Massive mounds of greater tussock-sedge (*Carex*

A local orchid of rich-fen grasslands is early marsh-orchid.

paniculata) stride across such sites and sometimes in the valley bottom, a strip of alder or sallow carr occurs. The best ones have remained open with cattle grazing. Within its acre or so of herb-rich turf at least 14 different sedge species can be found in one field at Kingcombe. Other interesting plants of these fenny, peaty sites include water avens (*Geum rivale*), marsh valerian (*Valeriana dioica*), early marsh-orchid (*D. incarnata*) and very occasionally marsh helleborine (*Epipactis palustris*). Several local mosses occur typically in these restricted and now precious sites.

A high water table, even seasonal flooding, together with base-rich water provides the conditions for another type of neutral grassland now rare in Dorset. This is the turf of the flat flood plains of the chalk streams, like the Frome and Piddle and their tributaries. Here the combination of naturally productive soil and an abundant supply of constant relatively warm and rich water was once used to construct water meadows. At its peak some 200 years ago, this grassland management depended on taking water from the chalk river in leats, to feed channels on slight ridges across the fields, and allowing this water to trickle across the turf, draining off in the gulleys and back to the river. This flush of warm, rich water encouraged an early bite of spring grass, providing a valuable and timely supplement to the feeding of the huge flocks of sheep pastured across the downland landscape of southern England in the seventeenth and eighteenth centuries.

The grassland was carefully managed, even hand-weeded to remove coarser and less palatable species, including many herbs, so a turf dominated by grass resulted. No examples of this water meadow system are now worked in Dorset though the valley flood plains still bear many traces of the sluices, carriers and the slightly ridged surface so characteristic of this ingenious land use. These can be easily spotted from the roads across the Frome valley at Dorchester for instance. Even though permanent pasture sometimes remains, the level ground and natural productivity have meant that almost without exception the grassland has been improved by herbicides and fertilisers, even if ploughing has not occurred. A few examples have been partly abandoned and now support rich fen vegetation, and one or two examples survive of the grassland type that probably preceded the water meadow management throughout many of our valleys.

Vast numbers of sheep were grazed on the southern chalk downs and their water meadows in the chalk stream valleys, then folded with hazel hurdles on arable land to fertilise it with their droppings – 1930s.

Few examples of flood meadow with abundant marsh marigold survive in the river valleys, like this area of Wareham Common.

On part of Wareham Common can be seen an area of turf beside the lower Piddle that stays wet in spring after winter flooding and which, for a few brief days, boasts an unusual abundance of marsh marigolds (*Caltha palustris*) in the sward. Several grasses comprise the turf with a number of other herbs, like lady's smock (*Cardamine pratensis*) and ragged robin, together with the frequent presence of the inconspicuous, creeping brown sedge (*Carex disticha*). The site is grazed by cattle and horses, completing a portrait probably typical of the grassland that once extended over much of the flood plains of the chalk rivers, away from acidic drainage from the heaths, before such water meadows were intensively managed or 'improved' by modern agriculture. There are only tiny fragments of this type of neutral grassland left and the few acres at Wareham Common, not consumed by the by-pass, are probably the largest such area in Dorset.

There is even less grassland of high nature conservation value on acidic soils in Dorset than survives on neutral soils. This has probably always been the case, since markedly acidic soils are rather more limited in extent than the great bands of broadly neutral clay soils that once supported herb-rich turf. Many of the acid soils are poor and free-draining, or in contrast totally water-logged, and only able to support heather-dominated heathland or mire. These internationally renowned communities have been described in a companion volume in this series, *Heathlands*.

Where the conditions are not so extreme, or where there has been a history of grazing, acid grassland communities do still grow, sometimes as a gradation from dwarf-shrub heath, sometimes on the edges of mires and flushes, and sometimes as a distinct but usually localised grassland type. The main areas in Dorset are thus the acidic soils of the heathland basin in the south-east and the Greensand hilltops typical of west Dorset. But locally patches of clay-with-flints on the top of some of the chalk downs can support pockets of heathy grassland. The same is true of the Bridport Sands, such as in the wonderfully sinuous valleys south of Poorton. Here the steep slopes have made cultivation impossible, encouraging an attractive but rather species-poor turf of acid grassland.

Perhaps because these acid grasslands tend to have less diversity they have been seen as poor examples of heathland, or semi-improved neutral pasture, and until recently their conservation has been largely ignored, but the best of them are amongst the most exciting for scarce species of any of our grasslands. Typically, the turf's main grasses will be sheep's fescue and common bent, with others like sweet-vernal grass and Yorkshire fog also frequent. Sheep's sorrel (*Rumex acetosella*) is abundant, especially on the drier sites prone to drought, perhaps with heath bedstraw (*Galium saxatile*), pill sedge (*Carex pilulifera*), green-ribbed sedge (*C. binervis*) and field woodrush (*Luzula campestris*). In general, agricultural improvement has been the main cause of loss, but, in south-east Dorset, the lack of heathland grazing has allowed coarse vegetation and scrub to thrive at the expense of the finer turf. In one rare surviving example of grazed turf,

The Valley of Stones National Nature Reserve near Little Bredy has chalk downland slopes with acid heathy grassland on the hilltops; and the finest example of a 'train' of sarsen stones in Dorset.

bordering heathland, there is a clutch of scarce species, including smooth cat's-ear (*Hypochaeris glabra*), clustered and subterranean clovers (*Trifolium glomeratum*) and (*T. subterraneum*), pale dog-violet (*Viola lactea*) and mossy stonecrop (*Crassula tillea*). The resumption of grazing on a number of the Dorset heaths may allow this rich medley of plants to flourish again.

On acid hilltops, on the downs and over Greensand, heathy grassland which includes heathers and bilberry (*Vaccinium myrtillus*) may still be found, together with many of the grasses and herbs of acid turf. Bristle bent grass (*Agrostis curtisii*), purple moor-grass and wavy hair-grass (*Deschampsia flexuosa*) also thrive, the latter only in the west of Dorset since it is strangely absent from the main heathland area of the south-east. Such acidic patches are often small, giving way within a few paces to chalk grassland, as at the Valley of Stones and near Flower's Barrow. In a few other spots, localised screes of leached chalk and flint pebbles occur, again with an acid grassland character and often with typical heathland lichens and mosses. Melbury Down in the north of the county has some fine examples of this unusual community.

The most extensive acid grassland site in Dorset, and probably one of the finest in the country, is Corfe Common, a remarkable working common dotted with tumuli and the later hollow-ways, formed during Corfe Castle's heyday at the heart of the medieval stone trade in Purbeck. The long continuous history of cattle and pony grazing, and its location on the mildly acidic wealden sands and clays, are the keys to Corfe Common's richness. To these must be added the frequent occurrence of springs and flushes, all of them combining to create a habitat remarkable for numerous notable plants and several very scarce insects. Masses of wild chamomile (*Chamaemelum nobile*); acres of saw-wort, betony and devil's-bit; heath, marsh and spotted orchids; bog pimpernel (*Anagallis tenella*) and pale butterwort (*Pinguicula lusitanica*); adder's-tongue and bitter-vetch (*Lathyrus linifolius*) – these and many, many other gems abound on the Common.

The ancient grazed acid grassland of Corfe Common has many local flowers in abundance, including betony (*left*) and in the damp flushes, bog pimpernel.

Several populations of the southern damselfly (*Coenagrion mercuriale*) are the reason why Corfe Common is now also a site of European importance. Happily, their future seems secure now that the National Trust is maintaining the vital grazing and tackling invading scrub and bracken. Some of the original Common was reclaimed in the Second World War and has remained as improved grassland. The Trust is slowly restoring it, a task that takes time. This can best be seen on the few acres that were ploughed in wartime and returned to Common management after the war. Even now, though within exactly the same grazing regime, it lacks several of the herbs so abundant in the undamaged turf alongside.

Corfe Common has both wet and dry acid grassland. There are interesting elements of wet acid communities, often in intimate mixtures with other grassland types, in some of our river valleys, where the influence of acidic drainage from the heaths meets the base-rich water of the chalk streams. Good examples of this occur at

The only population of the strangely named viper's-grass occurs in wet acid grassland within grazing marsh near Wareham.

Some of the small flushes around Corfe Common support one of our rarest
dragonflies, the southern damselfly.

Wareham Common, the Moors and at Tadnoll. Frequent components
of the turf in such sites are purple-moor grass, lousewort and meadow
thistle, together with several sedges and jointed rush. Bottle sedge
(*Carex rostrata*), marsh cinquefoil (*Potentilla palustris*) and bogbean
(*Menyanthes trifoliata*) are typical along the ditch edges, while very
locally great burnet (*Sanguisorba officinalis*) and whorled caraway
(*Carum verticillatum*) may be found. It is in one of the two places
where whorled caraway can be seen that viper's-grass (*Scorzonera
humilis*) grows regularly in its only locality in England.

So our grasslands have their share of nationally rare and scarce
species, but most interesting is the range of grassland communities
that exist, each reflecting some subtle change in soils, ground water
and past management. Sadly, even now the few remaining hectares of
unspoiled grassland remain under threat, but the great upsurge in
habitat recording and a better awareness of the richnes – and scarcity
– of our surviving grasslands should encourage further conservation of
this superb element of our natural heritage in Dorset.

ACCIDENT OR DESIGN?

There is, of course, a substantial resource of small grassland sites that exist more by accident than for their primary purpose of providing grazing or hay. These are the road verges, railway banks, and churchyards of Dorset. Nonetheless the contribution that these grasslands can make to nature conservation must not be ignored, especially when the 'real' grasslands have been so reduced. Few of these accidental survivals are more pleasant than the setting of some of our lovely ancient churches.

Many of the medieval churches were built on open pasture land – the common fields of the medieval manor, so that today their churchyards may represent small patches of surviving ancient grassland set within the more heavily farmed landscape or the town houses that now surround them.

Churchyard grasslands can span both damp and drier areas, furnishing suitable habitats for a wide range of plants. The surrounding hedges and trees, particularly the traditionally planted churchyard yew, provide miniature woodland habitats, whilst the church walls and gravestones have become one of the most rewarding places to find lichens on a surprising variety of rock types.

Churchyards are traditionally managed by regular mowing to maintain a tidy appearance. However, the nationally run 'Living Churchyard Project', set up to promote interest in wildlife in churchyards, has encouraged a re-assessment. Under the guidance of the Dorset Wildlife Trust some 50 churches have so far become involved. By mowing certain areas less regularly a wide range of native plants can be encouraged to flower, providing enjoyment as well as nectar for butterflies and other insects. If this is carried out with care, and with neatly mown paths, the attractive appearance and wildlife richness of the churchyard can be enhanced.

Plants which frequently occur in churchyards throughout the

Ancient grassland with wild daffodils is the tranquil setting
for Holwell church.

county include once widepread species that have been lost from many
areas, such as cowslips, bird's-foot-trefoil, ox-eye daisy, bugle (*Ajuga
reptans*), rough hawkbit, lady's bedstraw and heath bedstraw. One
churchyard for instance has a glorious spring display of wild daffodils,
whilst sharp-eyed visitors to another can find a succession of unusual
flowers, including early purple, spotted and twayblade (*Listera ovata*)
orchids, dyer's greenweed, knapweeds, fleabane (*Pulicaria
dysenterica*) and corky-fruited water-dropwort.

For lichens, the church walls and gravestones take the place of the
bare rock surfaces found on natural exposures like coastal cliffs but
with the huge advantage of a close mixture of basic and acidic rock
monuments! Because of the considerable age of many church buildings
and headstones, lichens have had centuries to colonise them. Many of
the lichens are widespread but some are rare. One such species only

occurs on crumbling lime mortar, and is in danger of extinction every time repairs are carried out! Rare or common though, the lichens impart a wonderful patina to the stonework of our churchyards, enhancing the age and attractiveness of the mellow stone they colonise. So far, nearly a hundred Dorset churchyards have been

Flowery grassland with ox-eye daisies, cut in late summer and old gravestones encrusted with lichens.

The strange lizard orchid is one of our rarest plants –
and it grows on a roadside verge.

surveyed for lichens: a quarter have over 70 different types, whilst five have more than 100 species.

Rather less peaceful than the reflective quiet of the churchyard, another accidental survival of grassland is to be found on the many miles of road verges, some ancient relics of old pasture, some newly created.

Some years ago the Dorset Wildlife Trust started a project to record the verges of greatest interest to wildlife, paying particular attention to less common plants. It now has a register of over a hundred prime verges, varying in length from 10 metres to 2 kilometres. Dorset County Council has been notified of these sites and manages them in co-operation with the Trust. They are clearly marked to enable verge-cutting contractors to follow specific advice about when to cut, allowing rarer plants to seed. Plants that benefit from this treatment include the rare narrow-leaved lungwort (*Pulmonaria longifolia*), which grows locally in the south-east of the county, spiny restharrow (*Ononis spinosa*) and the lizard orchid (*Himantoglossum hircinum*), our largest native orchid, which although rare has the intriguing habit of appearing in surprising places. Our one small colony continues to defy the traffic on a narrow verge two metres from a busy main road and in a site that is by no means an ancient grassland.

The road verge project needs constantly updating as local conditions change, and regular information on the health of the verges is crucial. It is something of an irony that protection from too frequent cutting and the economies of the highway authority may now be the greatest threat to many of our road verge plants. A single cut, all too often late in the year can mean that the verge steadily becomes dominated by a few coarse species rather than the range of less competitive plants for which it was registered. The verge of the Swanage road beside Corfe Common is an example where I have seen the variety of fine plants decline over the years.

The county also has a number of unusual heathland verges in the south, where plants requiring an alkaline soil can surprisingly be found a few metres from heather and other associated acid-loving plants. This unusual combination is almost certainly due to the use of

Marsh helleborine is a local orchid of rich-fen grassland.
It occurs on some damp road verges where limestone
may have been used to form the road base over peat.

The kestrel is a bird very frequently seen hunting over the long grass of road verges, to spot insect or small mammal prey.

limestone or chalk, which was originally laid down as hardcore for tracks over the soft peaty soils on parts of the wet heath. Plants that can be found on these verges include bee and pyramidal orchids, kidney vetch and dropwort (*Filipendula vulgari*)*s*. The margin of the Ferry Road between Studland and Shell Bay is typical whilst the verges of the small road out to Arne are famous for this unusual feature. Sadly the greater volumes of traffic even on these small roads lead to vehicles driving onto the turf, so changing its composition, or the imposition of kerb stones that all too often means disturbance and the arrival of enriched, alien topsoil.

Another distinctive type of road verge occurs most noticeably across the Blackmore Vale. Here often very wide verges, somewhat out of scale with the narrow road, survive between the big hedges. These may be survivals of the great drove roads that existed long before the tarmac road came.

There are also a few examples of new verges where a deliberate attempt has been made to create a feature of nature conservation

Left Damp grassland in river valleys or the transition to upper saltmarsh are the typical habitats of the lesser marsh grasshopper.
Right The rapidly increasing long-winged conehead was very rare only a few years ago but now is found in a variety of places with long grass.

The three common grasshopper species, common green (*Omocestus viridulus*), meadow (*Chorthippus parallelus*) and common field (*C. brunneus*) may be found in many grasslands, including gardens as well as more special sites. The common green is the first to be heard in early summer and, like the meadow grasshopper, is perhaps most at home in lusher grass. The drier grasslands are favoured by the common field grasshopper, whose typical buff and fawn colours match the dried grass leaves of high summer. There are more spectacular colour forms to look out for though, including a stunning pink variant!

Another grasshopper frequently seen in certain grasslands, though traditionally characteristic of heathland, is the small mottled grasshopper (*Myrmeleotettix maculatus*). It is more strongly patterned than normal forms of the three common species and has either green or brown as its main colour. A particularly attractive green and grey form is good camouflage for the mottled grasshopper on open stony grassland sites like the sparse, lichen-rich turf of some downland tops, as at Bindon Hill.

Well grazed, warm downland slopes are the favourite habitat of the neat stripe-winged grasshopper (*Stenobothrus lineatus*), which is locally frequent in suitable sites in Dorset. The woodland grasshopper (*Omocestus rufipes*) is even more localised, restricting itself to the

The very rare and elusive mole cricket may still occur in damp grassland over sandy soils.

longer grass of the woodland edge and other transitional sites. Where the lusher river valleys merge into saltmarsh is where to find the larger, evenly coloured lesser marsh grasshopper (*Chorthippus albomarginatus*).

Though difficult to see and even harder to hear, two slender bush crickets – the long-winged and short-winged coneheads (*Conocephalus discolor*) and (*C. dorsalis*) – are not uncommon, though nationally they are quite scarce. Until 1983 the long-winged conehead was very rare, but its rapid expansion from a few coastal flush sites into heathland in Dorset was noted at the same time as a similar increase in the New Forest. It has now spread right across southern England, occurring in longish grass in grassland as well as heathland sites, while the short-winged conehead prefers damper grassland with rushes.

In contrast the decidedly chunky wart-biter cricket (*Decticus verrucivorus*) lives at only one site in Dorset. It is one of our rarest insects and is found otherwise only in Sussex and Wiltshire on single chalk downland sites with a mix of long and short flowery turf. The single Dorset population is on a mosaic of heath and acid grassland which provides shelter in the dwarf shrubs and food from the herb-rich patches of turf, a habitat maintained by grazing in one of the National Nature Reserves. Perhaps rarest of all, as well as the largest

Much more restricted and needing longish turf with big cowslip plants, often associated with scrub edge, is duke of burgundy.

grow big, duke of burgundy (*Hamearis lucina*) may be found and holly blue (*Celastrina argiolus*) and green hairstreak (*Callophrys rubi*) will be happy. On short, open turf on hot slopes, but alas on few Dorset sites, silver-spotted skipper (*Hesperia comma*) may be seen. In complete contrast, the rank tor grass turf of ungrazed sections of the coastal chalk and limestone is the home of the Lulworth skipper (*Thymelicus acteon*). Given its local abundance it is easy to forget that in England it is only found on Dorset's coastal grasslands.

MAMMALS

Many of our mammals are seen in grassland and it may form an important part of their range, though other habitats like woodland or hedgerows are also essential. Longer turf can often support large populations of field voles (*Microtus agrestis*)and long-tailed field mice (*Apodemus sylvaticus*), and this in turn can provide one of the most appealing sites of grassland – though not for the voles! – a barn owl (*Tyto alba*) hunting at dusk. The activities of moles (*Talpa europaea*)are obvious in grassland, and of importance in providing open patches and assisting drainage. The brown hare (*Lepus*

Cowslips on the steep chalk slopes of the Dorset Wildlife Trust nature
reserve at Fontmell Down.

protected sites throughout the county. Conservation ownership and
management of grassland sites has also increased in recent years.

We have in Dorset approximately 5000 hectares of grassland with
a high conservation value. Half of the grassland Sites of Special
Scientific Interest are on chalk and limestone. These tend to be of a
larger size than the remaining neutral and acid grassland areas, which
in most cases have become even more fragmented.

The National Trust has continued to acquire important grassland
on chalk, limestone and clay, especially near the coast, but the
acquisitions have also been inland, as the impressive continuous tract
of downland at Fontmell and Melbury Downs south of Shaftesbury
illustrates. Another very important and impressively large expanse of
grassland, on the coastal limestone of Purbeck is of European

Above Part of the National Trust's great sweep of limestone downland on the Purbeck coast near Worth Matravers and managed by extensive grazing with hardy cattle and ponies.
Opposite page Adder's Plot, one of the unimproved meadows at Kingcombe Farm in west Dorset.

significance. This is the area that runs east from Seacombe to Dorset County Council's outstanding site at Durlston. There are now National Nature Reserves on chalk grassland at Hambledon Hill and at Hogcliff near Maiden Newton, with the newest NNR designation at the Valley of Stones. The Dorset Wildlife Trust's portfolio of important grasslands continues to expand, with small but very rich sites at Corfe Mullen and Bracketts Coppice following the inspirational acquisition of unimproved farmland at Lower Kingcombe Farm in west Dorset. That bold move in 1987 caught the imagination of the nature conservation world and, as well as safeguarding the largest tract of traditionally managed neutral grassland surviving in Dorset, doubtless inspired other Wildlife Trusts to follow suit.

Whilst ownership by a nature conservation body may often be of critical importance, especially to save a site from certain change, many grassland fragments will continue to remain in private hands. Whatever the ownership the survival of grassland for wildlife will

Cutting hay at Kingcombe. Relatively modern machinery replicates the traditional practices (*see opposite page*) that have persisted for centuries.

depend on continuing favourable management. The days of massive reclamation with grants to do it are probably gone for ever. Perhaps the biggest threat today is neglect. Without annual grazing or cutting and removal of the year's crop of herbage, the grassland quickly becomes rank and dominated by a few coarse species like false oat-grass (*Arrhenatharum elatius*) or cock's-foot (*Dactylis glomerata*). Imagine the lawn left for a few seasons without the routine mowing! The great number of smaller, less aggressive species including almost all of the typical herbs of interesting grassland are quickly suppressed. After a few years they may not even survive in the seed bank in the soil. The tendency for scrub and trees to take over is also clear. Bramble or gorse usually establish first, but trees are equally quick in taking advantage of the lack of cropping, so that in a few years a thicket and eventually a new wood emerge.

There is a tension here for nature conservation. Surely trees are good and we need more, not fewer? But the secondary woodland that would grow if left to its own devices is no substitute for the richness of ancient woodland, rightly seen as a habitat of outstanding value, and the grassland lost to scrub and trees would be a serious further loss of an already scarce and depleted natural resource. Positive intervention for nature conservation is essential, by cutting scrub and keeping a grazing or cutting system in place. The big threat comes when the grassland fragment no longer plays its traditional role in the farming system. We must have all seen isolated steep downland banks, once part of an extensive grazing pattern, but now islands in arable land. No animals can reach the bank to graze; indeed the farm possibly no longer has any stock. The grass bank is doomed and often as not its fate is further sealed by deliberate tree planting.

It is an irony that even some conservation sites have suffered such a loss, for fear that cutting or grazing of the flowers would stop the treasured objects setting seed. However, grassland has been managed by summer grazing and cutting for centuries. Grassland herbs and grasses are adapted to this regime; indeed they depend on it. Most of the component species are perennials that do not need annual recruitment from seed, and in any case most will manage to set seed from a late flowering or from the many individual plants that don't get

Grassland management, such as this traditional hay-making in the 1890s at Winterborne Monkton, means regular cutting or grazing and grassland plants depend on such practices.

One of the most successful recent examples of restored grassland, at Powerstock, where forestry plantations have been removed to allow flower-rich acid and and neutral turf to return.

cropped. The converse is sadly all too obviously poor for the conservation of grasslands. We do not need to look far to see for instance that road verges long protected from their routine cut, change all too readily to coarse grass and cow parsley. So do not despair to see a hayfield cut at the height of its flowering, or grazing happening on downland throughout the summer. Far from being damaging, these are the very traditional practices that have maintained our few surviving grasslands of conservation interest throughout the centuries.

VISITING DOWNS, MEADOWS
& PASTURES

As this book has described, the rich grassland areas that survive in Dorset are mostly managed by conservation bodies or lie in the MOD training area. The former are usually accessible on foot, the latter at advertised periods on designated paths. In addition to the major sites listed below, road verges, cuttings and some churchyards offer rewarding sights for the grassland enthusiast.

Key: BC: Butterfly Conservation, DWT: Dorset Wildlife Trust, DCC: Dorset County Council, EH: English Heritage, EN: English Nature, M.O.D.: Ministry of Defence (Army Ranges), NT: National Trust, PL: Plantlife, PDC: Purbeck District Council.

BADBURY RINGS, NEAR WIMBORNE (SY 965030) [NT]. Iron Age Hill Fort on Kingston Lacy Estate off the Wimborne – Blandford B3082 road by the Beech Avenue. Rich downland flora – including 13 species of orchid – on the Rings and surrounding land. Easy flat access from NT car park. No dogs because of grazing animals.

BALLARD DOWN AND GODLINGSTON HILL, NEAR SWANAGE (SZ 048812 Ballard Point), (055824 Old Harry Rocks), (013812 Godlingston Hill) [NT]. Superb downland walk from Old Harry to Ulwell. Cliff-top turf and steep south-facing grassy slopes above Whitecliff Farm. Whole area including Godlingston Hill renowned for butterflies. Access from Ulwell lay-by on Swanage – Studland road SZ 022808, via Whitecliff Farm 028808, or more distantly from south beach car park at Studland.

BROOKLANDS FARM CONSERVATION CENTRE, FORSTON, DORCHESTER (SY 666952). Headquarters of the Dorset Wildlife Trust. Demonstration wildflower meadow. Indoor exhibition and leaflets for nature reserves in the care of the Trust. Car park.

CORFE CASTLE COMMON (SY 960810) [NT]. Large area of rich acid and neutral grassland and of scrub in the heart of Purbeck. Fascinating management history. Access from village car park in West Street (958813) or near junction of A351 (Swanage) and B3069 (Kingston) south of village, at SY 965811.

CORFE MULLEN MEADOW (SY 980967) [DWT]. Small flower-rich meadow noted for green-winged orchids. Limited roadside parking.

CORSCOMBE MEADOWS, HALSTOCK LEIGH (ST 515065) [DWT]. Most attractive for summer flowers, part of Brackett's Coppice Nature Reserve [DWT]. See also Ryewater Farm below.

DURLSTON COUNTRY PARᴋ, SWANAGE (SZ 0317730) [DCC/PDC]. Renowned conservation area with wide variety of coastal wildlife interest including extensive limestone meadows carefully managed for flora and fauna. Visitor centre, guided walks and displays. Car park or walk up from downs above Swanage Pier.

EGGARDON HILL (SY 540946) [NT]. Rich chalk downland including part of Iron Age hillfort. Access north from A35 through Askerswell. Limited roadside parking east of hill at crossroads (547947).

FONTMELL AND MELBURY DOWNS (ST 884184 & ST 900193) [NT/DWT]. Large tract of magnificent chalk downland. Rich flora and exceptional butterfly populations. Carefully monitored grazing regimes coupled with scrub control. Small NT car park at 886186.

GOLDEN CAP ESTATE, CHARMOUTH (SY 383934) (Stonebarrow Hill) [NT]. Coastal estate with largest area of undamaged neutral grassland in Dorset. Best meadows are those on Upcott and Westhay farms. Both flora and insect fauna exceptionally rich. Remember the estate is made up of working farms with the meadows grazed and/or cut for hay. Access off A35 up narrow lane to Stonebarrow car park. Self-guided walks.

GREENHILL DOWN, NEAR MILTON ABBAS (ST 792037) [DWT]. Secluded nature reserve of chalk downland and coppiced wood above Milton Abbas. Access by public footpath from Hilton village. Very limited parking by church at 782030 (avoid obstructing church access).

HAMBLEDON HILL, CHILD OKEFORD (ST 845125) [EN - NATIONAL NATURE RESERVE]. Extensive chalk downland varied in slope and aspect. Impressive elongated hillfort dominates the skyline. Excellent English Nature leaflet covers flora, butterflies and management. Run in partnership with organic farm. Bridle and footpaths give access from Child Okeford (West) and Shroton (East) ends of hill. Limited parking off Duck street and Shaftesbury Road, near Child Okeford or in Shroton (Iwerne Courtenay) village.

HOD HILL, NEAR BLANDFORD (ST 8571070 [NT]. Closely adjacent to Hambledon Hill. Large square Iron Age hillfort, with Roman fort in NW corner. Rich flora and butterfly interest. Access along bridleway from north end of Stourpaine village (limited parking) at 861099, or from lay-by on minor road towards Child Okeford, nr. Hanford.

HOG CLIFF, NW OF DORCHESTER (SY 620970) [EN - NATIONAL NATURE RESERVE]. Chalk grassland, scrub and coppice reserve astride the main A37 Dorchester – Yeovil road. Access from lay-by on A37 at South Field Hill on foot and bridle paths, or from road along Sydling valley. Leaflet available.

KINGBARROW QUARRY, PORTLAND (SY 692732) [DWT]. Fine example of old quarry with limestone grassland, flowers and butterflies. Access from car park behind Portland Heights Hotel.

KINGCOMBE MEADOWS, TOLLER PORCORUM (SY 545985) [DWT]. Dorset Wildlife Trust's Lower Kingcombe Farm untouched by modern agriculture, 'the farm that time forgot'. Superb range of rich meadows with flora varying according to soil, dampness and aspect. Visitor centre with small car park at Pound Cottage (554990). Also limited parking at Clift (546984). Approach off A356 Maiden Newton – Crewkerne road through Toller Porcorum. Visitors welcome but must recognise that Kingcombe is a working farm. Guided walks and residential courses offered by the nearby Kingcombe Centre (555991).

KNOWLTON RINGS, NEAR CRANBORNE (SZ 023102) [EH]. Small circular henge enclosing a ruined church. Rich chalk flora on banks. By Wimborne – Cranborne B3078 road.

LORTON MEADOWS, NEAR WEYMOUTH (SY 674826) [DWT]. Unimproved neutral grassland with small areas of woodland siuated in valley between Upwey and Littlemoor near Weymouth. Interpretation Centre in restored barn (opening winter 2003). Toilets. Access via Lorton Lane off A354 and from Upwey Railway Station (½ mile).

LOSCOMBE, NEAR POWERSTOCK (SY 506982) [DWT]. Steeply sloping pasture with small wetland rich in marsh orchids. Limited parking opposite Rose Cottage. Access by public footpath.

LULWORTH M.O.D. RANGES (SY 882802 Tyneham). Large sweep of coastland downland used for gunnery training. Continuous M.O.D. use since World War Two has prevented the downland being ploughed or exposed to agricultural chemicals. Famous for the Lulworth skipper butterfly. Extends from Lulworth east to edge of Kimmeridge Bay. Access limited to waymarked paths during 'opening times' mainly week-ends and summer holiday season. (Details published locally in advance). Car parking at Tyneham (also Visitor Centre), Lulworth Cove and Kimmeridge Bay. Outstanding chalk grassland sites at Bindon Hill, Flowers Barrow, Gad Clifftop, and Whiteway Hill. Remember this is a danger area and safety considerations are paramount.

MAIDEN CASTLE (SY 668885) [EH]. Iron Age hillfort sw of Dorchester. Rich chalk flora and fauna on banks and surrounds. Access from car park at 669889.

MAIDEN NEWTON WATER MEADOWS (SY 592980). Private ownership. Example of former managed water-meadow system on River Frome now undergoing restoration. Access from Rockpit Farm car park 593979.

MUCKLEFORD, NEAR DORCHESTER (SY 642931) [DWT]. Disused chalk pit with rich grassland flora. Off A37 near Stratton crossing R. Frome. Limited parking by bridleway.

PORTLAND QUARRIES (Inc Broadcroft and Perryfields Quarries) (SY 697722 & 691713) [BC]. Fine limestone grassland and butterflies (in particular the cretaceous form of the silver-studded blue butterfly).

POWERSTOCK COMMON (SY 540973) [DWT]. Predominantly woodland this large Reserve includes an increasing area of acid grassland restored from forestry and a contrasting old railway cutting with a chalk grassland flora. DWT leaflet. Car park at Reserve entrance by disused railway bridge at 547974.

RYEWATER FARM, NEAR CORSCOMBE (ST 515065) [PL]. Large farmland area including pasture, hay meadow and stream. See also Corscombe Meadows [DWT] above.

SOVELL DOWN, NEAR CRANBORNE (ST 992108) [DWT]. Small chalk grassland and scrub area on the Ackling Dyke with rich flora. Limited roadside parking at 994109.

SPYWAY FARM AND SEACOMBE, LANGTON MATRAVERS (SY 984770 – SY999778) [NT]. Magnificent limestone grassland slopes on south Purbeck coast. The central section of a long sweep of downland between Durlston (see above) and St. Aldhelm's Head. Early spider orchid abundant. Car parking at end of Durnford Drove. Small NT centre at Spyway Barn 999778.

STOBOROUGH HEATH, NEAR WAREHAM (SY 937864) [EN]. Heathland reserve but with large areas of dry and wet acid grassland being restored from agriculture. Small car park at Sunnyside at grid reference above. Leaflet available.

STONEHILL DOWN, NEAR CHURCH KNOWLE (SY 925822) [DWT]. Chalk downland, scrub and woodland on the backbone of the Purbeck Hills, west of Corfe Castle. Rich flora especially on the south-facing valley slopes. Limited parking near Creech Barrow at 922822.

TADNOLL, NEAR WINFRITH (SY 792873) [DWT]. Large Reserve with wet acidic meadows beside the heathland. Managed in conjunction with Winfrith Heath [dwt]. Limited roadside parking at GR above.

TOWNSEND, NEAR SWANAGE (SZ 024782) [DWT]. Limestone grassland over disused quarries filled with scrub. Now linked to Durlston CP (see above) to create extensive plateau of limestone grassland managed for conservation. Park at Herston or walk from Durlston CP.

TURNWORTH DOWN AND OKEFORD HILL (ST 810085) [NT] Okeford Hill. Picnic Site (812093). [DCC]. Chalk downland and woodland including Iron Age settlement (Ringmoor). Car parking on Okeford Hill. Walk along Wessex Ridgeway to NT gateway.

VALLEY OF STONES, NR. LITTLE BREDY (SY 595880) [EN}. Mix of chalk and acid grassland with clear traces of Celtic fields and fine 'train' of sarsen stones. Very limited parking at Little Bredy. Leaflet available.

WAREHAM COMMON (SY 918878) Good example of winter-flooded pasture by River Piddle once typical before 'improvement' of neutral grassland elsewhere. Park in Wareham (Streche Road Park) and use signed path for Wareham Two Rivers Walk and Wareham Forest Way towards West Mills. (Other Wareham meadows east of town by River Frome).

WEST BEXINGTON, NR. ABBOTSBURY (SY 527866) [DWT]. Coastal site behind Chesil bank including wet meadow. Park in West Bexington car park at 531864.

WHITENOTHE, NR. WEYMOUTH (SY 765810) [NT]. Western end of superb sweep of coastal downland from Durdle Door to Ringstead Bay including The Warren and Bat's Head. Access from NT South Down car park above Ringstead Bay 760824.

FURTHER READING

Ash, H., Bennett, R., Scott, R., *Flowers in the Grass* (English Nature) 1992 (A booklet mainly dealing with the creation of flower-rich grasslands).

Bowen, J., *The Flora of Dorset* (Pisces Publications) 2000 (Full and up to date records of the entire county flora including lower plants and with brief descriptions of the main habitat types including grasslands).

Crofts, A. & Jefferson, R., *Lowland Grassland Management Handbook* (English Nature/Wildlife Trusts) 1999 edition (Loose-leaf folder packed with detailed management information; and with a very full list of further reading including reference to many research papers).

Cunliffe, B., *Wessex to AD 1000 – a regional history of England* (Longman) 1993 (Discusses the agricultural origin and early management of habitats).

DERC, *Dorset Chalk Grassland Inventory,* 1998; *Dorset Acid Grassland Inventory,* 2002; *Dorset Neutral Grassland Inventory,* 2002 (The most up to date and comprehensive distribution of all known surviving fragments of importance).

Duffey, E., Morris, M., Sheil, J., Ward, L., Wells, D., Wells, T., *Grassland Ecology & Wildlife Management* (Chapman Hall) 1974 (A collection of scientific accounts of many aspects of grassland fauna and flora including many invertebrate groups and the effects of management).

English Nature, *Old meadows and pastures* 2002; *Lowland calcareous grassland* 2001; Nature Conservancy Council, *The conservation of cornfield flowers* 1989 (Free colour leaflets with simple accounts of the national resource of each of these habitats).

Hillier, S., Walton, D., Wells, D., *Calcareous Grasslands – Ecology & Management* (Bluntsham Books, Huntingdon) 1990 (A further, more recent and more specific series of scientific papers on the effects of management on some grassland fauna).

Hubbard, C., *Grasses* (Penguin) 1984 (Only black & white drawings and with some names changed, but still a classic).

Jermy, A., Chater, A. & David, R., *Sedges of the British Isles* (BSBI) 1982 (Also black & white drawings but detailed and with clear descriptions).

Lousley, J., *Wildflowers of Chalk & Limestone* – New Naturalist 16 (Collins) 1969 (An interesting historical record of downland flora before the main period of agricultural change. But very sparse on Dorset's downs!).

Marshall, J. & Haes, E., *Grasshoppers & Allied Insects of Great Britain & Ireland* (Harley Books) 1988 (Probably the best comprehensive cover but distributions of this group have changed!).

Pearman, D., *Sedges & their allies in Dorset* (DERC) 1994 (Excellent account of distributions and habitats with some tips on identification).

Pinder, C., Wallis, S. & Keen, L., *Dorset from the Air* (Dorset Books) 1995 (A good selection of aerial photos showing the frequent link between good archaeological and nature conservation sites; and how much has been lost!).

Price, E., *Lowland Grassland & Heathland Habitats* (Routledge) 2003 (Very up to date and readable account).

Rodwell, J., *British Plant Communities 3 – Grassland & Montane* (CUP) 1992 (The National Vegetation Classification – a classic scientific description of all of the main grassland types in Britain and their distribution).

Rose, F., *The Wildflower Key* (Fred Warne) 1981 (One of many floras and not the latest, but with very good tips to identification).

Rose, F., *Colour Identification Guide to Grasses, Sedges, Rushes & Ferns* (Viking) 1989 (Again one of several, more focussed floras with clear illustrations).

Tansley, A., *The British Islands & their Vegetation* (2 volumes) (CUP) 1953 edition
Britain's Green Mantle George (Allen & Unwin) 1949 (Classic descriptions of the major semi natural vegetation types and their history).

Thomas, J. & Webb, N., *Butterflies of Dorset* (DNH&AS) 1984 (Good account of county distributions and habitat needs though again some will have changed).

ACKNOWLEDGEMENTS

I am indebted to the many friends and colleagues, past and present, who have helped me to identify and appreciate the beauty and fascination of our native grasslands. Some who taught me the craft of field botany are sadly deceased now – Peter Wanstall and Derek Wells in particular; others whose enthusiasm and energy are an inspiration, are still very much part of the Dorset natural history scene, such as David Pearman and Bryan Edwards. And there are those friends of a little further back who so generously shared their knowledge of Hampshire – Michael Bryant, Fay Stranack and Graham Darrah for instance.

I am very grateful to the Dorset Wildlife Trust for the invitation to write the original chapter on *Grasslands* in *The Natural History of Dorset*, from which this book grew. And I am especially grateful to Tony Bates, Colin Varndell and my old acquaintance Bob Gibbons, for the use of their stunning photographs.

Most of all I am indebted to my dear friend Rob McGibbon who has so often shaken me out of weekend laziness to visit and discover over many years, Dorset's wildlife hotspots and throughout has been unfailingly such good company.

These friends and many others have helped me to understand and interpret grasslands, but they were merely my inspiration; any mistakes are my own work!

I am grateful to the following for allowing the use of illustrations in their possession or for which they hold the copyright: Tony Bates; front cover, pages 19, 21, 25, 34, 38, 40, 62, 68: Dorset County Museum; page 17 (bottom): Dovecote Press; pages 37, 52, 67: Bob Gibbons; pages 4, 7, 10, 11, 13, 15, 16, 17 (top, both), 21 (all), 22 (both), 23, 24, 26, 28, 30 (all), 31, 32, 36, 41 (both), 42, 43, 45, 46, 47, 48, 51, 54 (both), 55, 56 (bottom, both), 59, 63, 64, 66; Colin Varndell; frontispiece, pages 33, 35, 49, 53, 57, 58, 61 (all), 65: Peter Wilson (Natural Image); 50, 56 (top).

The map on page 8 was kindly provided by the Dorset Environmental Record Centre.

INDEX

The

DISCOVER DORSET

Series of Books include

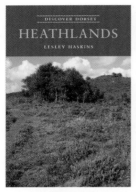

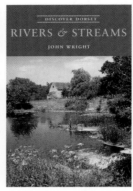

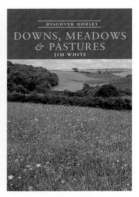

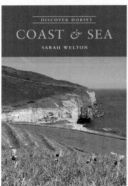

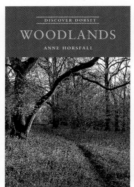

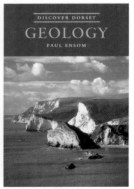

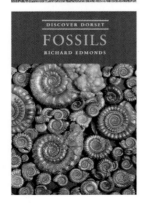

All the books about Dorset published by
The Dovecote Press
are available in bookshops throughout the
county, or in case of difficulty direct from the
publishers.
The Dovecote Press Ltd, Stanbridge,
Wimborne, Dorset BH21 4JD
Tel: 01258 840549
www.dovecotepress.com

Contents

Introduction

'The richest man on earth is poor if he is jealous. God save us all from jealousy.'

Othello is a happy man. A brave soldier who has fought in many wars, he is now a general. The Duke of Venice needs him in his wars against the Turks, and the people of Venice love him. Now Othello also has a personal reason to be happy. He has fallen in love with Desdemona, a beautiful and clever young woman, and she loves him with all her heart.

But there are problems in Othello's life, too. He is fighting the Turks, but he is an outsider in Venice; he is a black man from north Africa. Desdemona's father, Brabantio, welcomed him to his house as a friend, but he doesn't want a black husband for his daughter. And Othello has some enemies – men like Roderigo, who wanted to marry Desdemona.

Luckily Othello has good friends, soldiers like himself: Michael Cassio, his lieutenant, for example, and Iago, his ensign. Othello thinks that Iago is a wise and honest man. He always believes what Iago tells him. When Iago tells him an unpleasant story about his new wife, what should Othello do? Who can he believe – his friend or his wife? Is Iago the honest man he seems? Or is he playing an evil game with Othello's mind?

Othello is one of Shakespeare's best-loved plays, and is still full of meaning for us today. It shows us a man who is good – even great. And it shows how an evil man can destroy him. Othello makes one terrible mistake; he believes the wrong person. He is told lies, and these change him. He becomes more and more jealous, and by the end of the play the good, brave man has become very dangerous.

This is a dark story, with little hope in it. Good people suffer and die for their mistakes. At the heart of the story there are many questions that we still ask ourselves today: Can we really love people who are different from us in some way? Why does one man want to destroy another? Are some people simply evil? Why is jealousy sometimes so strong? How can love change so quickly into hate?

Shakespeare wrote about twenty other plays before *Othello*. He was about forty years old and already a well-known actor and writer when he wrote it, in 1603 or 1604. As he usually did, he took an earlier story for his play. The story of Othello comes from Giovanni Battista Giraldi's *Ecatommiti* (*One Hundred Tales*, 1566).

Othello is still popular in the theatre. Verdi also put the story to music for his *Otello*, and there have been many films made. One famous film was made by Orson Welles in the United States in 1952. Welles also plays Othello. In 1965 the famous British actor Laurence Olivier was a very successful Othello, both at the National Theatre in London and in a film, with Maggie Smith as Desdemona. It seems strange now that in the past the part of Othello was so often played by a white actor. That has now changed, and in Oliver Parker's 1995 film, the black actor Laurence Fishburne played Othello.

William Shakespeare (1564–1616) is the most famous writer of plays in the English language. He was born in Stratford-upon-Avon in England. He went to a good school, but did not go to university. In 1582 he married Anne Hathaway and they had three children. By 1592, he was in London; there he acted in plays and wrote them. In the next twenty years he wrote thirty-seven plays and many poems. He sometimes wrote three plays in one year. His plays were very popular, and many of them were acted in front of Queen Elizabeth I and, later, King James I.

Reading and acting the play

You can read *Othello* silently, like every other story in a book.
You will have to imagine the places, the people's clothes and
their voices from the words on the page.

But Shakespeare did not write *Othello* as a story book to read
at home. He wrote it for actors on a theatre stage. You can read
the play in a group with other people. This is very different from
silent reading. You can speak the words and bring the people in
the play to life. They can sound happy or sad, worried or angry.
You can add silences or noises, like the sound of guns. You can
also stop and discuss the play. What does this person mean? Why
does he/she say that?

But you can have more fun if you act the play. *Othello* has a
lot of exciting scenes, and also some quiet, personal times. The
people in the play have to show a lot of different feelings. If
you act the play, you can show these feelings by your words and
actions.

The story happens in the streets, houses and palaces of Venice
and Cyprus. You should find out what those places looked like.
You should also think about the clothes that the people in the
play wear. Some of them are soldiers, but rich and important
people had beautiful, brightly-coloured clothes. The men wore
swords, and you will have to plan some fights. In some scenes
many people come onto and leave the stage; in others, two
people talk softly together; and sometimes there are songs or
short poems.

Othello is an important play, and everyone can enjoy it and
learn from it. Have fun with it!

The People in the Play

OTHELLO, a Moor; a general, fighting for Venice
DESDEMONA, Othello's wife
CASSIO, Othello's lieutenant
IAGO, Othello's ensign
EMILIA, Iago's wife
BIANCA, Cassio's lover
RODERIGO, a young Venetian, in love with Desdemona

THE DUKE OF VENICE
BRABANTIO, a rich Venetian, Desdemona's father
GRATIANO, Brabantio's brother
LODOVICO, Desdemona's cousin
MONTANO, an important man in Cyprus

OFFICER, under the Duke
1ST OFFICER, under Montano
2ND OFFICER, under Montano
A MESSENGER

SOLDIERS
SERVANTS

Act 1 Love and War

Scene 1 A street in Venice

[*Roderigo and Iago are walking along the street together.*]

RODERIGO [*angrily*]: Iago, I thought we were friends. You happily spend my money, but you knew …

IAGO: Why don't you listen to me? I didn't know about it.

RODERIGO: Do you really hate him? Can I believe that?

IAGO: Of course I do! Three of the most important men in this city wanted to make me his lieutenant, but he refused to listen. 'I've already picked my officer,' he said. And who was the chosen man? Michael Cassio! A man who has never even been to war. And what job do I get after all my years as a soldier? I'm an *ensign*, that's what! The Moor's* *ensign*. Now, Roderigo, tell me, do I love him or do I hate him?

RODERIGO: So why are you working for him?

IAGO [*laughing*]: Oh, don't worry! I have my reasons. My face doesn't show what's in my heart. [*stopping and pointing*] Look! Here's her father's house. Why don't we wake him up and destroy his happiness?

RODERIGO [*shouting*]: Brabantio! Signor† Brabantio! Wake up!

IAGO: Thieves, Brabantio, thieves! They are robbing your house, stealing your daughter and your money.

[*Brabantio opens an upstairs window and looks out.*]

BRABANTIO [*angrily*]: What's the matter? Why are you shouting?

RODERIGO [*sounding worried*]: Are all your family at home, sir?

---

* Moor: the name used at the time for a man from North Africa
† Signor: the Italian for Mr or sir

BRABANTIO: Why do you ask?

IAGO [*sounding very worried*]: Bad news, sir, bad news. Your heart will break when you hear it. An old black cat has your little white bird in his mouth. Get up, before it's too late!

BRABANTIO: What are you talking about? Who's there?

RODERIGO: Sir, don't you know my voice?

BRABANTIO: Oh, so it's *you*. You are not welcome here, Roderigo. I've been honest with you. You can't marry my daughter.

RODERIGO [*politely*]: Sir, sir, please listen. We only want to tell you …

IAGO [*very roughly*]: Your daughter is riding a big black horse. Do you want grandchildren with black tails and four legs?

BRABANTIO: What's that? What are you telling me?

IAGO: Oh sir, the Moor. Your daughter is with the Moor.

BRABANTIO [*angrily*]: What? Lies! You'll pay for this!

RODERIGO: Sir, please tell us, have you given permission for your daughter to marry the Moor? If not, your daughter is giving herself to a stranger. Is she in her room?

BRABANTIO [*frightened*]: Call my servants! Bring lights! This is my worst dream. Oh, what shall I do if it is true! Light, I say, light! [*He goes away from the window to search his house.*]

IAGO: I must leave you now, Roderigo. I can't safely speak against the Moor yet. He is the best general we have in our war with the Turks. The people love him. Bring Brabantio's men to the bar called the Rose. I will be there with him. Goodbye.

[*He leaves. Brabantio runs out into the street in his night-clothes, followed by servants with lights.*]

BRABANTIO [*to Roderigo, sounding heart-broken*]: It's true. She's gone, and my life is at an end. Where did you see her, Roderigo? With the Moor? How could she do this to her father? [*to the servants*] Bring more lights! Oh, my heart! How did she get out? Fathers – never believe your daughters! [*to Roderigo*] Did he use magic, Roderigo? Is it possible?

RODERIGO: Yes, sir, I think it is.

BRABANTIO: Call my brother! Oh, Roderigo, why didn't I give her to you ... Do you know where they are?

RODERIGO: Yes. Bring your men and follow me.

BRABANTIO: Take me to them. [*to the servants*] Call more men! Bring your swords!

Scene 2 *The street outside the Rose*

[*Othello and Iago are standing in the street talking. Servants are holding lights.*]

IAGO: I have killed men in times of war, but I could not murder him. Sometimes, I think I'm too soft. I should kill him.

OTHELLO: No, no. It's better this way.

IAGO: Oh, you don't know the terrible things he said about you. I hated listening to them. Tell me, sir, are you already married? If not, Brabantio will try to stop you. He's an angry man.

OTHELLO: Oh, he can try ... I have helped Venice win a war, and I come from a family of princes. I am as proud and successful a man as Brabantio. I loved my free life at sea, but now I love his daughter Desdemona more. What are these lights? Who's coming? Is it Brabantio?

IAGO: No, I don't think so.

[*Cassio comes along the street, with men carrying lights.*]

OTHELLO: The Duke's servants and Cassio, my lieutenant! Good evening, friends. What's the news?

CASSIO: The Duke needs you immediately, General. Messengers have arrived with news of the war, and they've all been searching for you.

OTHELLO: Good. I must speak to someone here for a minute, and then I'll go with you. [*He goes into the Rose.*]

CASSIO: Iago, what's he doing here?

IAGO: He's taken a great ship, but on land, not at sea.

CASSIO: I don't understand.

IAGO: He's married.

CASSIO: What? Who is she?

IAGO: It's [*seeing Othello*] – wait!

[*As Othello returns, Roderigo and Brabantio walk towards them. With the new arrivals are officers carrying lights.*]

CASSIO: General, here are some more people who want to speak to you.

OTHELLO [*to Roderigo and Brabantio*]: Stop there!

RODERIGO [*to Brabantio*]: Signor, it's the Moor.

BRABANTIO [*shouting at Othello*]: You thief!

IAGO [*pulling out his sword*]: Roderigo? Stand there and fight me!

OTHELLO: Stop! Put away your swords. [*sounding friendly*] Signor Brabantio, we do not need to fight.

BRABANTIO: Thief! What have you done with my daughter? You have used magic on her. She has refused to marry so many fine young men here in Venice. She could never love a black man like you! I'll throw you into prison for this.

OTHELLO: Stop! I won't fight you. Look, the Duke's messengers are here. He needs to see me on some urgent business.

BRABANTIO: What? The Duke? At this time of night? Then I'll speak to him, too.

[*They all leave.*]

Scene 3 The Duke's palace

[*The Duke and officers are sitting around a table, with lights, and servants standing around them. A messenger comes in.*]

DUKE: What news?

MESSENGER: More Turkish ships, my lord. They are attacking Cyprus. Signor Montano asks you to send help.

'Thief! What have you done with my daughter?'

DUKE: We must do something quickly. [*Brabantio, Othello, Iago, Roderigo and other officers come into the room.*] Brave Othello, we must send you to war immediately. You must sail against our enemies, the Turks. Brabantio – welcome. We have missed your wise words this evening.

BRABANTIO: My lord, forgive me. I am not here because of the Turkish attack. I have trouble of another kind.

DUKE [*surprised*]: Why? What's the matter?

BRABANTIO [*crying out*]: My daughter! Oh, my daughter!

DUKE: Dead?

BRABANTIO: Yes, dead to me. A thief has stolen her from me with his evil magic.

DUKE [*angrily, standing up*]: Who is this man? He will suffer for this.

BRABANTIO: My lord, I thank you. [*He points at Othello.*] Here is the man – this Moor!

DUKE: I am sorry to hear this, Othello. What do you say?

OTHELLO [*calmly*]: My lord, it is true. I have taken this old man's daughter. True, I have married her. I cannot speak fine words. I'm just a soldier. But I can tell you the story of my love for Desdemona and how I won her heart.

BRABANTIO: My daughter is a quiet, shy girl. She can't love this man. He has used magic on her – I know it!

DUKE [*quietly*]: You believe that, but it may not be true.

OFFICER: Tell us, Othello. Did you use magic on the girl, or did her love for you come naturally?

OTHELLO: Please, my lords, send a servant to the Rose. Bring the lady here. If she doesn't love me – then take away my life.

DUKE [*to his servants*]: Bring Desdemona here.

OTHELLO: Iago, take them to her. You know the place best. [*Iago and some servants go out.*] While we wait, I will tell you the story of our love.

DUKE [*sitting down*]: Tell us, Othello.

OTHELLO: Her father was a friend to me and often invited me to their home. He asked me to tell him about my life. I told him everything. I have seen war on land and sea. I spoke about terrible accidents and wonderful adventures, great danger and greater successes. I have known strange countries where the mountains touch the sky. I have seen men with heads that grow below their shoulders. Desdemona loved listening to my stories. Then she began to love me for my stories, and I loved her for that. My lord, that is my only magic – the story of my life.

[*Desdemona, Iago and the servants arrive.*]

DUKE: What do you say now, Brabantio? Othello has explained everything. Do you believe him?

BRABANTIO: Desdemona, come here and tell us. What do you want?

DESDEMONA: Dear father, you have given me life, and I must love you as a daughter. [*looking at Othello*] But here's my husband. My mother left her father and followed you. Now I must follow the Moor.

BRABANTIO [*coldly*]: Goodbye, then! Come here, Moor. I give you my daughter. [*He gives Othello her hand.*] I do not want to lose her, but you have already taken her from me.

DUKE: Brabantio, don't be angry. If a robbed man smiles, he steals something from the thief. We can't always change things, but we can hide our sadness. But now let us talk about the war. The Turkish ships will soon reach Cyprus. Othello, you know that island. You must forget your new happiness for some time, and sail to war.

OTHELLO [*proudly*]: I am a soldier, and I know war best. I am glad to go. But, please, find a safe and comfortable place for my wife while I am away.

DUKE: Her father's house is the best place for her.

BRABANTIO [*coldly*]: No. She can't go there.

OTHELLO: I agree. That is not the right place for her.

DESDEMONA: And I agree, too. If Othello goes to sea, I must go with him.

OTHELLO: Please give her permission to come, my lord. I'm not a young man, thinking of love. I'm going to sea to fight our enemies. I will never forget that. But I need her with me.

DUKE: You can decide, Othello. But this is an urgent matter, and you must leave tonight.

DESDEMONA [*surprised*]: Tonight, my lord?

OTHELLO: With all my heart.

DUKE: Men, we'll meet again at nine in the morning. Othello, leave an officer here to bring your wife to you.

OTHELLO: My lord, I choose Iago, my ensign, for that job. He is a good and honest man. I will leave my wife with him. He can bring her, with messages from you.

DUKE: Excellent! Good night to you all. [*to Brabantio*]
Brabantio, try to see what others can.
Othello's black – but a good man.

BRABANTIO [*to Othello*]:
Oh Moor, you think your love is true.
But as she's done to me, she'll do to you.

[*The Duke, Brabantio, officers and servants all leave the room.*]

OTHELLO: Never! [*to Iago*] Honest Iago, I must leave Desdemona with you. Ask your wife to look after her. Come, Desdemona, my love. We have only an hour together before I leave.

[*Othello and Desdemona leave.*]

RODERIGO: Iago!

IAGO: What, friend?

RODERIGO [*crying*]: Oh, what shall I do?

IAGO [*impatiently*]: Go to bed and sleep.

RODERIGO: I shall kill myself.

IAGO: What are you talking about? Kill yourself for a woman?

A dog in the street has more sense!

RODERIGO: What can I do? My heart is broken.

IAGO: Your heart! What is that? We must follow our heads, not our hearts and our hot blood. [*laughing*] And that's what love is − just hot blood.

RODERIGO [*sadly*]: You're wrong.

IAGO: No, I'm not. [*roughly*] Be a man! Kill yourself? Never! Remember, I'm your friend. I'm here to help you. [*seeming to remember*] But you'll need money. Desdemona won't love the Moor for ever, and he won't love her. It started quickly, and it will end quickly, too. Then you'll need money in your purse. Be patient, and you will have her. [*putting his arm around Roderigo*] But money − you'll need that. We'll talk again tomorrow at my house.

RODERIGO: I'll be there.

IAGO [*warmly*]: Good man! No more talking about death, do you hear me?

RODERIGO [*quietly*]: No. I've changed.

IAGO: Goodbye. Oh, and put some money in your purse!

RODERIGO: I'll sell all my land. [*He leaves.*]

IAGO [*to himself*]: Excellent work! I'll soon have his money. It's the only reason I spend time with a man like him. Oh, it's almost too easy. I hate the Moor. Some people say he's my wife's lover. Is it true? I don't know − but I'll finish him. He likes me − good! [*laughing*] That makes my job easier. Now, how will I do it? Here's an idea. I'll use Cassio, and bring *him* down, too. Cassio likes women, and they like him. Perhaps he's a little too friendly with Desdemona. I must tell Othello. He'll believe me, because I'm Iago, his honest friend. That's it! I have my plan.

Now deepest hell and blackest night
Will take away the day's clear light.

Act 2 A Storm and a Fight

Scene 1 *Cyprus, near the sea*

[*Montano and some of his officers are looking out to sea.*]

MONTANO: What can you see?

1ST OFFICER: Nothing. The weather is too wild.

MONTANO: The waves are like mountains. Ships are easily lost in this weather.

[*Another officer comes to talk to them*]

2ND OFFICER: News, my friends! Our wars with the Turks are at an end. They have lost their ships in the storm.

MONTANO [*excited*]: Is this true? How do you know?

2ND OFFICER: A ship has arrived from Venice. Michael Cassio, lieutenant to the brave Moor, Othello, is here. Othello is still at sea, on his way to us.

MONTANO: I hope he is safe. I know Othello. He is a great man.

[*Cassio comes to them.*]

CASSIO: Thank you, good men of Cyprus, for your kind words about the Moor. Oh, God help him! I lost him on a wild and dangerous sea.

MONTANO: Does he have a good ship?

CASSIO: Yes, his ship is strong, and he has fine sailors with him. I still hope to see him safely on land. [*Voices call: A sail! A sail!*] What's that?

1ST OFFICER: The town is empty. All the people are at the beach. They've seen a ship!

CASSIO: I hope it's Othello's!

[*There is the sound of guns.*]

10

2ND OFFICER: Guns! That means it's a friendly ship, not an enemy.

CASSIO: Please see who it is.

2ND OFFICER: I'll go now. [*He goes.*]

MONTANO: Lieutenant, is your general married?

CASSIO: Yes. He has found a wonderful wife – the perfect woman for him. [*The 2nd officer returns.*] Who's on the ship?

2ND OFFICER: It's Iago, the general's ensign.

CASSIO: He is very lucky. Even the screaming winds and rough, rocky coast do not want to hurt the beautiful Desdemona.

MONTANO: Who is she?

CASSIO: The lady I told you about – our general's wife. Iago is looking after her and bringing her to her husband. Please God, protect Othello's ship and bring him safely to land.

[*Desdemona, Emilia, Iago, Roderigo and servants arrive.*]

CASSIO: Look! They are here! Let us fall to our knees to welcome this lady to Cyprus. [*He goes down on his knees.*]

DESDEMONA: I thank you, brave Cassio. What news do you have of my lord Othello?

CASSIO [*standing*]: He is not here yet, but he will arrive soon.

DESDEMONA: Oh, but I feel afraid! How did you lose him?

CASSIO: The storm carried my ship away from his. [*Voices call: A sail! A sail!*] But listen! The people can see a ship!

1ST OFFICER: I can hear guns. This is a friendly ship, too.

CASSIO: Go and get the latest news. Iago, good Ensign, welcome to Cyprus. Welcome, Emilia. Let me kiss your wife, Iago. In Florence we always greet our friends like this. [*He kisses Emilia on the mouth.*]

IAGO: Oh, be careful, sir. Her tongue never stops moving.

DESDEMONA: But Emilia is saying nothing.

IAGO: She usually talks too much. I can't sleep because of it. I hear her voice even when she is silent.

EMILIA [*hurt*]: You are unkind to me.

DESDEMONA: Don't listen to your husband, Emilia. Cassio, isn't he terrible?

CASSIO [*smiling, taking her hand*]: Remember, lady, he's just a soldier.

IAGO [*to himself*]: He's taking her hand. Yes, touch her. Yes, smile at her, kiss her hand. Excellent! It all helps me to destroy you. [*There is the sound of shouting.*] [*to the others*] The Moor! He's coming!

DESDEMONA [*excited*]: Let's hurry to meet him!

[*Othello and some soldiers come in.*]

OTHELLO [*holding out his arms*]: Oh, my Desdemona!

DESDEMONA [*running to him*]: My dear Othello!

OTHELLO [*taking Desdemona in his arms*]: How wonderful it is to see you, my dearest wife. If you are there after every storm, I welcome the wild winds and waves. If I die now I will die happy.

[*They kiss.*]

IAGO [*to himself*]: Oh, you are making sweet music now, but soon you'll sing a different song.

OTHELLO: Friends, the wars are at an end. The Turks have gone. Their ships are all destroyed. How are all my old friends here? Come, Desdemona. It's wonderful to be here with you.

[*They all go, except Iago and Roderigo.*]

IAGO: Come here, Roderigo. Are you a brave man? Well, they say love makes men brave. Listen. Cassio is our chief guard tonight, and I must tell you this. Desdemona is in love with him.

RODERIGO [*very surprised*]: With him? That isn't possible!

IAGO: She loved the Moor because he told her a lot of silly stories. He isn't handsome or young, and she'll soon grow tired of him. It's natural! She'll look around for another man, and who will she find? Cassio! He's young, good-looking – everything that women like. In fact, she's after him already.

RODERIGO: I can't believe that of her. She isn't like that.

'My dear Othello!'

IAGO: Not like that? She's a woman, isn't she? And a woman who's loved the Moor. Didn't you see her hold Cassio's hand?

RODERIGO: She was just being polite.

IAGO: No she wasn't! Didn't you see how close she put her face to his? Listen, sir. Stay awake tonight. Wait outside the guardhouse. Cassio doesn't know you. He'll come out of the guardhouse. Then you must find a way to make him angry.

RODERIGO: Why? I don't understand.

IAGO: Sir, he gets angry very easily. He'll hit you. Good! We want him to! Then he'll be in trouble. They'll throw him out of Cyprus. Then I'll be able to help you. You'll get what you want.

RODERIGO: I'll do it.

IAGO: Good! I promise you success. Meet me later, and we'll talk more about this. [*Roderigo leaves.*] I believe that Cassio does love her. And it's possible that she loves him. I know the Moor loves her. He is a loving, kind man – but I hate him. Now, *I* love Desdemona, too – or I want to have her. Why? I think the Moor has had my wife. So I will either take his wife or destroy him with jealousy. That's why I need Roderigo. First I must destroy Cassio. I fear he's been running after Emilia, too. I'll destroy him, and the Moor will thank me for my good work. [*He laughs.*] Then I'll drive him crazy.

Scene 2   The soldiers' guard-house

[*Othello is talking to Cassio. Desdemona is with him, and some servants.*]

OTHELLO: Good Michael, you will be chief of the guards tonight. Cyprus is safe and it will be a happy night for everyone. Some people will drink too much. Make sure there is no fighting.

CASSIO: Iago knows what to do. But I will watch the guards personally.

OTHELLO: Iago is an honest soldier. Good night, Michael.

14

[*to Desdemona*] Come, my dear love.
After the wind and rain the sea is calm;
Tonight I'll hold my sweet wife in my arms.

[*Othello, Desdemona and the servants leave. Iago comes in.*]

CASSIO: Welcome, Iago. We must guard the town together.

IAGO: Not yet, Lieutenant. It's too early. Our general is in a hurry to get to bed with his new wife. We can understand why. She's a lovely woman.

CASSIO [*seriously*]: She is a very fine lady.

IAGO: And I'm sure she enjoys the game of love.

CASSIO: She is a fresh, sweet girl.

IAGO: Even her voice seems to call for love.

CASSIO: Yes, she is perfect.

IAGO: Well, I hope they're happy together. Come, Lieutenant. I have some wine, and our friends will soon be here. We'll all drink to the health of black Othello and his new wife.

CASSIO: Not tonight, good Iago. I can't drink much. It's sad, but I have a weak head for wine.

IAGO: Oh, just one cup. This isn't an ordinary night. Your friends need you to drink with them.

CASSIO: Where are they?

IAGO: Here at the door, already. Call them in.

CASSIO: Well, I'll do it, but I fear… [*He goes out.*]

IAGO [*to himself*]: Some good men of Cyprus are on guard tonight. They've already drunk a lot. When Cassio is with them, trouble is sure to follow. Ah, here they come.

[*Cassio comes in with Montano, some other officers and servants with wine.*]

CASSIO: They've given me a cup of wine already.

MONTANO: Only a little one, a very little one!

IAGO: Bring more wine! [*He sings.*]

15

> A soldier's life is very hard
> He has no time to think.
> So open up a bottle, boys
> And give the men a drink!

CASSIO: An excellent song, my dear old friend. I drink to the health of our general!

IAGO [*singing*]:

> Oh, hold your wine cups high
> And let us drink them dry.
> This life is so fine
> If we have enough wine –
> So hold your wine cups high!

CASSIO: This is a better song than the other!

IAGO: Shall I sing it again?

CASSIO: No. I don't want to go to hell. I must not drink any more.

IAGO: True, good Lieutenant.

CASSIO: Well, enough of this. We must guard the town. I am not drunk. This is my ensign and this is my right hand and this is my left. I can stand. And I can speak. Yes, I'm not drunk at all! [*He leaves.*]

MONTANO: Let's all go to guard the town.

IAGO: You see how Cassio is, Montano? He's a good soldier, but he always drinks too much. I hope he won't do anything stupid.

MONTANO: You should tell Othello about this. Perhaps he doesn't see it. Be honest with him about Cassio's problem.

IAGO: Oh no. I couldn't do that. Cassio's my friend. [*cries of: Help! Help!*] What's happening? [*Roderigo runs in. He is followed by Cassio, holding his sword.*]

CASSIO: Fight, man!

MONTANO: What's the matter, Lieutenant?

CASSIO: He says I'm drunk! I'll kill him!

RODERIGO [*very frightened*]: Kill me?

CASSIO: Quiet, you dog! [*He hits Roderigo with his sword.*]

MONTANO [*taking Cassio's arm*]: Stop, good Lieutenant!

CASSIO: Take your hands off me! I'll kill you, too!

MONTANO: Stop! You *are* drunk!

IAGO [*quietly to Roderigo*]: Go! Shout and wake the town! [*Roderigo runs off.*] Good Lieutenant, put down your sword. Help! Stop, Lieutenant! [*Cassio wounds Montano.*] Montano! Help! Oh, God. Lieutenant, you're in big trouble now!

[*Othello comes in, with servants.*]

OTHELLO [*loudly*]: What is happening here?

MONTANO: Oh, God, I'm hurt. Look at all the blood! I'm dying!

OTHELLO [*shouting*]: All of you, stop! Listen to me!

IAGO: Lieutenant! Montano! The General's speaking to you.

OTHELLO: What is happening here? Are we becoming worse than our enemies, the Turks? What is the reason for all this shouting and fighting? Honest Iago, can you tell me?

IAGO: I don't know. These men are all good friends, but suddenly they started fighting. I didn't see how it began.

OTHELLO: Michael Cassio, can you tell me?

CASSIO [*quietly*]: Forgive me, my lord, I cannot speak.

OTHELLO: Montano, you are a good man. Why are you fighting?

MONTANO [*weakly*]: Othello, sir, I am hurt. My life is in danger. I can't say much. I was attacked. I had to fight.

OTHELLO: Now I am becoming angry. This island has been at war. The people were full of fear of a Turkish attack. And now the guards are fighting! Iago, you must tell me. Who began it?

MONTANO: You must tell him, Iago.

IAGO: I'll cut out my tongue before I'll hurt Michael Cassio. But I must be honest. General, it happened like this. I was talking to Montano. Then we heard shouts. We found Cassio and another man fighting. Montano tried to stop Cassio. I ran after the other man, but I lost him. That's all I know. Perhaps Cassio has done wrong, but he had a good reason for it, I'm sure.

OTHELLO: Iago, Cassio is your friend. You don't want him to suffer for this. But I must punish him. [*turning to Cassio*] Cassio, after this, you cannot be my lieutenant. [*Desdemona comes in, with servants.*] Look, the noise has woken my dear wife.

DESDEMONA: What's the matter, my dear?

OTHELLO: Nothing, my love. Come back to bed. [*to Montano*] We will send a doctor to you.

[*Servants carry Montano away.*]

OTHELLO: Iago, tell the people their streets are safe.
Come, Desdemona; soldiers live to fight.
We cannot always lie in bed all night.

[*Everyone leaves, except Iago and Cassio.*]

IAGO: Are you hurt, Lieutenant?

CASSIO [*very quietly*]: I am hurt to death.

IAGO: No, don't say that.

CASSIO [*sadly*]: My good name, Iago, I have lost my good name. The best part of myself is gone.

IAGO: I thought you were hurt! The General is angry with you now, but he'll soon forgive you.

CASSIO: No, I can't ask him to forgive me. How could I be so stupid! A drunken animal – that's what I am. Oh, wine is a devil! I'm not drunk any more, but now I hate myself.

IAGO [*warmly*]: Don't say that! It isn't the end of the world! Lieutenant, you know I'm your true friend. I'll tell you what to do. You know, our general's wife is now *his* general. He'll do anything she asks. Ask her to help you. She won't refuse.

CASSIO: That's a good idea. I will go tomorrow morning and ask Desdemona to speak for me.

IAGO: That's right, Lieutenant. I must go now to the guards.

CASSIO: Good night, honest Iago. [*Cassio leaves.*]

IAGO: How kind I am! And I am being honest. Desdemona is

a sweet person, and she will try to help Cassio. But there is a black devil in my heart. When Desdemona talks about Cassio to the Moor, I will speak, too. I will tell him she loves Cassio. Then Othello will begin to hate her. I will use her goodness to destroy them all. Now, I have two things to do. My wife must speak to Desdemona and ask her to help Cassio. And I must show Othello Cassio and Desdemona talking together –

Yes, that's the way.

The evil's growing stronger every day.

Act 3   A Jealous Man

Scene 1   Early morning, outside Othello's house

[*Cassio is waiting for Iago.*]

CASSIO: Greetings, Iago.

IAGO: Haven't you been to bed?

CASSIO: No. Iago, I need to speak to Desdemona. Emilia can help me with that.

IAGO: I'll send her to you. And I'll get the Moor out of the way. Then you'll be able to speak freely to Desdemona.

CASSIO [*putting a hand on Iago's arm*]: I thank you with all my heart. [*Iago goes.*] I never knew a better, more honest man.

[*Emilia comes in.*]

EMILIA: Good morning, good Lieutenant. I am sorry to hear about your troubles. Desdemona is asking Othello to forgive you. Wait a little and all will be well.

CASSIO: Emilia, I must speak to Desdemona. Can you help me?

EMILIA: Of course. Please come in. I'll take you to her.

CASSIO: A thousand thanks.

[*They leave.*]

19

Scene 2 In Othello's house

[*Desdemona, Cassio and Emilia are talking.*]

DESDEMONA: Good Cassio, I will do everything possible to help you. [*putting her hand on his arm*] Believe me, Cassio, you and Othello will soon be friends again.

CASSIO: Good lady, I will always be your true servant.

DESDEMONA: I know you will. You love my lord Othello, and he will soon forgive you.

CASSIO [*unhappily*]: But first he must punish me. He will send me away. Then he will forget me.

DESDEMONA: No, Cassio, that will not happen. I will talk to Othello about you day and night. I will die before I fail you.

[*Othello and Iago come in.*]

CASSIO: I must go, my lady. I feel uncomfortable here. I will leave you. [*He walks quickly away.*]

IAGO [*quietly, to himself*]: Ah! I don't like that.

OTHELLO: What?

IAGO: Nothing, my lord. Or if – no. Nothing.

OTHELLO: Was that Cassio I saw? Was he talking to my wife?

IAGO [*sounding surprised*]: Cassio? No, my lord, that man ran away when he saw you. And he looked guilty. It can't be Cassio.

OTHELLO: Yes, it was Cassio.

DESDEMONA [*coming and taking Othello's hand*]: My husband! I was talking a minute ago to someone you are angry with.

OTHELLO: Who do you mean?

DESDEMONA: Your lieutenant, Cassio! My dear lord, please forgive him. Cassio loves you and is a true friend to you.

OTHELLO: Was he here a minute ago?

DESDEMONA: Yes, he was. Oh, Othello, he is suffering so badly. It made me sad, too. Please call him to you and forgive him.

OTHELLO: Not now, sweet Desdemona, some other time.

DESDEMONA [*smiling at him*]: But soon?

OTHELLO: For you, my love, yes.

DESDEMONA: Will you do it tonight?

OTHELLO [*coldly*]: No, not tonight.

DESDEMONA: Please tell me when. Othello, it's Michael Cassio, your old friend! He often came with you to my father's house.

OTHELLO [*impatiently, pushing her away*]: Enough, Desdemona. I will never say 'no' to you. But please leave me alone now.

DESDEMONA [*surprised, to Emilia*]: Come with me, Emilia. I will do what my husband asks.

[*Desdemona and Emilia go. Othello watches them.*]

OTHELLO [*quietly*]: Excellent woman! How I love you! If my love for you ever dies, my life will be at an end.

IAGO [*sounding serious*]: My lord?

OTHELLO [*turning to look at him*]: What, Iago?

IAGO: Cassio went with you to visit Desdemona at her father's house. Did he know then that you loved her?

OTHELLO: Yes, he often took my love letters to Desdemona, and brought her letters to me.

IAGO [*suddenly sounding worried*]: Oh, did he?

OTHELLO: Yes. Are you surprised? Is he not an honest man?

IAGO: Honest, my lord? Yes, I *think* he is.

OTHELLO: You think he is? What does that mean? What are you telling me, Iago? I heard you say, 'I don't like that', when Cassio left my wife. Then you asked, 'Did Cassio know you loved Desdemona?' Why? What is worrying you? Tell me!

IAGO: My lord, you know I love you.

OTHELLO: I think you do. That is why I am so afraid. If you are worried, there is a good reason for it.

IAGO: I believe Cassio is honest.

OTHELLO: I think so, too.

IAGO: Well then, I think Cassio is honest.

OTHELLO: Iago, please tell me what you really think.

IAGO: My lord, I do not want to tell you. It's easy to make a mistake.

OTHELLO: Iago, as my friend, you must tell me.

IAGO: My good name, my lord, is the dearest thing I own. A thief steals nothing if he steals my purse. It was mine; now it's his. But if he steals my good name – well, then I'm lost.

OTHELLO: You must tell me, Iago.

IAGO: No, I can't.

OTHELLO [*shouting*]: You must!

IAGO: Please, my lord, don't be jealous. That is a sickness that eats men's hearts. Oh, how jealous men suffer!

OTHELLO: Oh, what pain is in my heart!

IAGO: The richest man on earth is poor if he is jealous. God save us all from jealousy.

OTHELLO: Why are you saying this? Do you think I am a jealous husband? I am not. My wife is beautiful, popular, loves to talk, sings and dances well. And she chose to marry me. Why should I be jealous? If there *is* a reason, you must tell me.

IAGO: I am glad to hear this. Now it is easier for me to speak. Watch your wife with Cassio.

OTHELLO: Can it be true?

IAGO: She fell in love with you and married you. And her own father knew nothing about it. You see how clever she is? But I must stop talking like this. I do it out of love for you.

OTHELLO: No, you are right to speak.

IAGO: I can see that you are worrying now.

OTHELLO: Not at all, not at all.

IAGO: That isn't what I want. Cassio's my friend. My lord, you are troubled, I can see.

OTHELLO [*clearly worried*]: Not really. I believe Desdemona is honest. But it is only natural …

IAGO: Yes, that's exactly my point. Was it natural for her to refuse to marry a young Venetian? Was it natural for her to choose you? But forgive me, I shouldn't talk like this.

OTHELLO: If you discover more, tell me. Ask your wife to watch Desdemona. Now leave me, Iago. [*Iago goes.*] Oh, why did I marry her? This honest man knows more than he says.

[*Iago comes back.*]

IAGO: My lord, please forget what I said. Wait a little before you bring Cassio back as your lieutenant. If Desdemona tries to help him – well, watch her. But she's innocent, I'm sure.

OTHELLO [*coldly*]: Leave everything to me.

IAGO: Once again, goodbye. [*He goes.*]

OTHELLO: This honest man understands people so well. If she is unfaithful to me, she must go. I chose this lovely woman to be my wife. But is she really mine? Do other men enjoy what belongs to me? Ah, she is coming. [*Desdemona and Emilia come in.*] How innocent she looks. I do not want to believe it …

DESDEMONA [*smiling warmly at him*]: My dear Othello, your dinner and your guests are waiting for you.

OTHELLO: No, I am wrong.

DESDEMONA: What did you say? Are you ill?

OTHELLO [*touching his head*]: I have a pain here, in my head.

DESDEMONA: It will soon go. Let me tie this handkerchief around it. [*She tries to tie it, but can't.*]

OTHELLO: Your handkerchief is too small. [*He pushes it away, and she drops it.*] Leave it. Come, I'll go to dinner with you.

DESDEMONA: I am sorry that you are not well.

[*Desdemona and Othello go.*]

EMILIA [*picking up the handkerchief*]: I'm happy to have this. It was Desdemona's first gift from the Moor. Iago has asked me a hundred times to steal it. But she always has it in her hand. She even kisses it and talks to it. I'll give it to Iago. I have no idea why he wants it.

'I am sorry that you are not well.'

[*Iago comes in.*]

IAGO: Oh, it's you. What are you doing alone here?

EMILIA: Don't be angry, I've got something for you.

IAGO [*coldly*]: Really? I don't think so.

EMILIA: Yes, really. What will you give me for that handkerchief?

IAGO [*suddenly sounding interested*]: What handkerchief?

EMILIA: The one the Moor gave to Desdemona!

IAGO: What? Have you stolen it from her?

EMILIA: No. She dropped it by accident, and I picked it up.

IAGO: Good girl! Give it to me!

EMILIA: Why? What will you do with it?

IAGO [*taking the handkerchief from her*]: Why should I tell you?

EMILIA: If it isn't important, give it back. [*She tries to take it but can't.*] Poor lady! She'll cry when she can't find it.

IAGO: Say nothing to her. Now go. Leave me alone. [*Emilia goes.*] I'll drop this in Cassio's bedroom and he'll find it. Little things like this feed jealousy. The Moor is changing already. The sickness is in his blood, and it will burn him like fire. [*Othello comes in. Iago hides the handkerchief and speaks more quietly.*] No more sweet sleep for Othello! No medicine can help you now.

OTHELLO [*clearly suffering*]: Oh, she is unfaithful to me!

IAGO: No, General, never say that.

OTHELLO [*shouting*]: Get away from me! You are killing me!

IAGO: What, my lord?

OTHELLO: When I knew nothing, nothing could hurt me. I could sleep, I could enjoy life. I did not taste Cassio's kisses in my wife's mouth. Oh, it is better not to know!

IAGO: I'm sorry to hear this.

OTHELLO: Oh, my quiet mind has gone for ever. Goodbye to happiness, goodbye to my life as a soldier, to my success in the wars. Othello is finished!

IAGO [*happily, to himself*]: Is this possible?

OTHELLO: Show me, Iago. I want to see the worst with my own eyes. If you cannot prove it, I will kill you.

IAGO [*sounding frightened*]: Oh, God help me! How wrong I was to be honest! In this world, no honest man is safe. I'll be no man's friend if this is the result.

OTHELLO: No, stop! You should be honest.

IAGO: I should be wise. I was stupid to be honest.

OTHELLO: My wife is faithful! No, she is not! You are right! No, you are wrong! Oh, I need to be sure! Her lovely name is now as black as my own face! I cannot live like this! I must know!

IAGO: I see, my lord, how much you are suffering. I'm sorry I ever spoke. Do you want to be sure?

OTHELLO: Want to be sure? I *will* be sure!

IAGO: Yes, but how? Do you want to see them in bed together?

OTHELLO [*crying out*]: Oh, the pain!

IAGO: It will be difficult to catch them like that. No – impossible. But I can tell you something.

OTHELLO: What?

IAGO: A few days ago I stayed the night at Cassio's house and slept in his bedroom. I had toothache and didn't sleep well. Cassio talks in his sleep. 'Sweet Desdemona,' he said, 'we must be careful. We must hide our love.' Then he took my hand and cried, 'Oh, sweet lady!' Then he cried, 'Oh, why did you marry the Moor!'

OTHELLO [*crying out*]: Oh God, God!

IAGO: He was only dreaming.

OTHELLO: But his dream was true!

IAGO: It may be.

OTHELLO [*very angry*]: I'll cut her into pieces!

IAGO: No, be wise. We aren't sure yet. She may be honest. But tell me this: have you seen a pretty piece of cloth, a red and white handkerchief, in your wife's hand?

OTHELLO: I gave it to her. It was my first gift to her.

IAGO: Ah. I didn't know that. I saw that handkerchief today. I'm sure it was your wife's. I saw Cassio clean his beard with it.

OTHELLO: Now I see it all. Oh, Iago, how she will suffer for this. One death is not enough; I will give her fifty. Now all my love is gone and my heart is full of hate.

IAGO: But wait …

OTHELLO [*shouting*]: Oh, blood, blood, blood!

IAGO: Be patient. You may change your mind.

OTHELLO: Never, Iago, never. I am like the ice-cold waves of an angry sea. Nothing can change me, nothing can stop me. Now I cry to God for blood. [*He falls to his knees.*]

IAGO: Don't stand up yet. [*He also falls to his knees.*] I promise here to help my lord Othello. My head, my hand and my heart are all his. I am with him, in the bloodiest of fights.

[*They both stand.*]

OTHELLO: I will not offer empty thanks, but ask you for something immediately. You have three days to kill Cassio.

IAGO: Then my friend must die. But please, let her live.

OTHELLO: That evil woman will go to hell. I must find a quick death for the lovely devil. Now you are my lieutenant.

IAGO [*quietly*]: I am yours, for ever.

[*Iago and Othello leave.*]

Scene 3 *In the street*

[*Desdemona and Emilia are walking.*]

DESDEMONA [*worried*]: Oh where did I leave that handkerchief, Emilia?

EMILIA: I don't know, my lady.

DESDEMONA: Well, I am lucky my Othello is not a jealous man.

EMILIA: Is he never jealous?

DESDEMONA [*smiling*]: Who? Othello? No, never.

EMILIA: Look, here he comes.

[*Othello comes in.*]

DESDEMONA: Now I will talk to him about Cassio. I will not take 'no' for an answer.

OTHELLO [*coldly*]: How are you, Desdemona?

DESDEMONA: Well, my good lord.

OTHELLO: Give me your hand. Your hand is warm, my lady.

DESDEMONA [*smiling*]: It is a young, happy hand.

OTHELLO: A free and hot hand, an open and giving hand.

DESDEMONA: The hand that gave you my heart. Now, Othello, your promise to me.

OTHELLO: What promise, my love?

DESDEMONA: I have sent a servant to bring Cassio to you.

OTHELLO: My eyes are watery. Lend me a handkerchief.

DESDEMONA: Here, my lord.

OTHELLO: Not that one. The pretty handkerchief I gave you.

DESDEMONA [*nervously*]: I have not got it with me.

OTHELLO: A wise old woman gave that handkerchief to my mother. That woman knew magic ways to keep a man's love. My mother gave it to me for my wife. You must never lose it. If you do, the most terrible things will happen.

DESDEMONA [*frightened*]: Is it true?

OTHELLO: It is. Look after it well.

DESDEMONA: Oh God! Then I am lost.

OTHELLO [*shouting*]: Have you lost it? Tell me!

DESDEMONA: Oh God! It is not lost. But if one day …

OTHELLO: Get it! Show it to me!

DESDEMONA: I can do that, my lord, but not now. Now I want to talk to you about Cassio.

OTHELLO: Get me the handkerchief.

DESDEMONA: You will never find a better man.

OTHELLO: The handkerchief!

DESDEMONA [*crying*]: Why are you doing this?

OTHELLO: Oh, the devil! [*He goes.*]

EMILIA [*very surprised*]: Is this man jealous?

DESDEMONA: I have never seen this before. There surely is magic in that handkerchief. I must find it again.

EMILIA: Men are full of surprises. First they are hungry and we are their meat. But when they are full they become sick of our taste. Look. Here are Cassio and my husband.

[*Iago and Cassio come in.*]

IAGO [*to Cassio*]: There's no other way. Go and ask her.

CASSIO [*to Desdemona*]: My lady, I hope once again to be Othello's friend. Please help me.

DESDEMONA [*sadly*]: Oh, good Cassio, I cannot help you today. You must be patient. I will try another day.

IAGO: Is my lord angry?

EMILIA: When he left us, a minute ago, he seemed strange.

IAGO: What can it be? I will go to him and find out the reason.

DESDEMONA: Please do. [*Iago goes.*] Perhaps some business in Venice or here in Cyprus is troubling him.

EMILIA: I hope you are right.

DESDEMONA: I gave him no reason to be jealous.

EMILIA: Men need no reason to be jealous. It is a sickness in their minds.

DESDEMONA: God save Othello from that sickness. I will go to him. Cassio, stay here. If I can, I will talk to him about you.

CASSIO: I thank you, my lady.

[*Desdemona and Emilia go. Bianca comes to Cassio.*]

BIANCA [*smiling*]: Greetings, my dear Cassio.

CASSIO [*kissing her*]: How are you, sweet Bianca? My love, I was on my way to your house.

BIANCA: And I to yours, Cassio. I haven't seen you for a week. Seven days and nights! It's a long time to a lover.

CASSIO: I'm sorry, Bianca. I have a problem that fills my head with troubles. I'll soon come to you again. Now, Bianca, take this handkerchief. [*He gives it to her.*]

BIANCA: What's this, Cassio? A gift from a new friend? [*angrily*] Ah, now I understand what's happening.

CASSIO: Silence, woman! [*more kindly*] You're jealous. You think another woman gave this to me. You're wrong.

BIANCA: Who does it belong to, then?

CASSIO: I really don't know. I found it in my room. I like it very much. [*smiling at her*] Can you copy it for me, sweetheart? Take it now, and leave me here.

BIANCA: Leave you? Why?

CASSIO: I'm waiting to see Othello. I want to see him alone. I'll see you soon, Bianca. [*He walks away from her.*]

BIANCA [*sadly*]: Well, I must be patient.

Act 4 The End of Love

Scene 1 A street in Cyprus

[*Iago and Othello are talking.*]

IAGO: A kiss doesn't matter.

OTHELLO: Doesn't matter?

IAGO: But if I give my wife a gift …

OTHELLO: What then?

IAGO: Then it belongs to her, my lord. It's hers and she can give it to any man.

OTHELLO: Her body is hers, too. Can she give that away?

IAGO: Oh, that's another question. But the handkerchief …

OTHELLO: Oh, the handkerchief. I cannot stop thinking about it.

You say he has it?

IAGO: Yes. And he says …

OTHELLO [*shouting*]: What has he said? Tell me!

IAGO: He says he … I don't know.

OTHELLO: What? What did he do?

IAGO: He was in bed …

OTHELLO [*screaming*]: He was in bed with her! With my wife! Oh, he must die for this crime! [*He falls down, shaking.*]

IAGO: Work well, my medicine! [*shouting*] Oh, my lord! My lord Othello! [*Cassio comes in.*] Oh, Cassio! My lord is sick.

CASSIO: Put something under his head.

IAGO: No, leave him to sleep. If he wakes he will scream and shout. Leave us now. I must talk to you later. [*Cassio goes.*] [*to Othello*] How are you, General? Do you have a pain in your heart?

OTHELLO [*sitting up*]: Are you laughing at me?

IAGO: Laughing at you? No, of course not.

OTHELLO: I am hurt in my heart.

IAGO: While you were sick, my lord, Cassio was here. He's coming back soon. Quickly! Hide here, by this door. When he comes, I'll question him about your wife. Watch him when he talks about her. But be patient, my lord. Be a man.

OTHELLO: Are you listening, Iago? I will be patient. But I will – are you listening? – I will have blood for this.

IAGO: You are right. But wait. Now you must hide. [*Othello hides in the doorway of a house.*] [*quietly*] Now I'll talk to Cassio about Bianca, a poor girl who sells her body for bread. The silly thing is in love with Cassio, but he just laughs at her. Here he comes. [*Cassio comes in.*] Othello will see his face and go crazy with jealousy. [*to Cassio*] Hello, Lieutenant. How are you?

CASSIO: I am not the lieutenant, and that is killing me.

IAGO: Keep asking Desdemona for help. That's the way to succeed. [*smiling*] It's a pity Bianca can't help you!

CASSIO [*laughing*]: Oh, that girl!

OTHELLO [to himself]: He is laughing already!

IAGO: Well, Bianca really loves you. She says you're going to marry her. Is it true?

CASSIO: Ha, ha, ha!

OTHELLO [angrily, to himself]: Oh, you look happy now …

CASSIO: Marry her? Marry a whore? What a joke! Ha, ha! She follows me everywhere. The other day, I was talking to some men. She came and put her arm around me.

OTHELLO: He is showing how she touched him.

CASSIO: She kissed my hand and cried, and pulled my arm.

OTHELLO: She pulled him into my bedroom! Oh, I will throw your nose to the dogs in the street!

[Bianca arrives.]

CASSIO: Bianca! Why are you following me?

BIANCA: Why did you give me this handkerchief? A girl gave it to you. And now you ask me to copy it for you! Here, take it! I don't want the thing! [She throws it at him.]

OTHELLO: My God, it is my handkerchief. My gift to Desdemona.

IAGO [to Cassio]: Run after her!

CASSIO: Yes, I must, or there'll be more talk about me!

IAGO: Will you eat at her house tonight?

CASSIO: Yes.

IAGO: I may see you there. I must talk to you.

CASSIO: I'll see you there, then. [He goes.]

OTHELLO [leaving the doorway] How shall I murder him, Iago?

IAGO: Did you see him laughing?

OTHELLO [putting his hands over his face]: Oh, Iago!

IAGO: And did you see the handkerchief?

OTHELLO: Was that mine?

IAGO: Yes! Your poor, silly wife gave it to him, and he's given it to his whore!

OTHELLO: I want to kill him slowly. My sweet, lovely wife! Oh,

'He is showing how she touched him.'

she must die tonight. My heart has turned to stone. Oh, but she is the sweetest lady! A wife for a king!

IAGO: That only makes her worse.

OTHELLO: Yes, you are right. Oh, but the pain in my heart, Iago!

IAGO: If you love her so dearly, you may forgive her.

OTHELLO: Forgive her! I will cut her to pieces! I must kill her tonight. I will not speak to her first. If I do, her lovely face may weaken me.

IAGO: Kill her in her bed, the bed where she wrongs you.

OTHELLO: Good, good! That idea pleases me!

IAGO: Leave Cassio to me.

OTHELLO: Excellent! [*They hear shouting.*] What is that?

IAGO: News from Venice, I think. [*Lodovico, Desdemona and some servants come in.*] Look, the Duke has sent Lodovico. And your wife is with him.

LODOVICO: God save you, General. The Duke of Venice greets you. [*He gives Othello a letter.*]

OTHELLO: I kiss his words. [*He reads the letter.*]

DESDEMONA: What's the news, good cousin Lodovico?

IAGO: I am glad to see you, Signor. Welcome to Cyprus.

LODOVICO: Thank you. How is Lieutenant Cassio?

DESDEMONA: Cousin, he and my lord Othello are not friends now. But you can help me to change that.

OTHELLO [*coldly*]: Are you sure of that?

DESDEMONA: My lord?

LODOVICO: Is something wrong between my lord and Cassio?

DESDEMONA [*warmly*]: Yes, and I want to put an end to it. Cassio is a great favourite of mine.

OTHELLO [*shouting*]: Silence!

DESDEMONA [*worried*]: My lord? Are you angry?

LODOVICO: Perhaps it's something in the letter. The Duke is calling Othello back to Venice. Cassio will stay here in his place.

DESDEMONA: I am glad to hear that.

OTHELLO: Are you? You devil! [*He hits her across the face.*]

DESDEMONA [*touching her face, very unhappy*]: There is no reason for this.

LODOVICO [*very surprised*]: My lord, I cannot believe you are doing this. Look at your wife. She's crying.

OTHELLO [*screaming at Desdemona*]: Get away from me, woman! Leave us!

DESDEMONA [*looking very pale but calm*]: I will go. I hate to see you angry. [*She starts to go.*]

LODOVICO: Please, my lord, call the lady back.

OTHELLO [*shouting roughly*]: Woman!

DESDEMONA [*turning back to him*]: My lord?

OTHELLO [*to Lodovico*]: Well, what do you want to do with her?

LODOVICO [*looking very surprised*]: Who? I, my lord?

OTHELLO: Yes. You asked me to call her back. Oh, she will do anything a man asks. Now she is crying. Well, I must go home. Yes, cry, woman! I will return to Venice. Away, woman! Get out! [*Desdemona goes.*] Cassio will have my place. [*to Lodovico*] Please come to dinner tonight, Signor. Welcome to Cyprus! [*He leaves.*]

LODOVICO: Is this the great Moor, the brave General who wins wars for Venice? Is he sick? Has he gone out of his mind?

IAGO: He is what he is. I can't say any more.

LODOVICO: He hit his wife! Is he often like this?

IAGO: I can't honestly tell you what I've seen here. You must watch him and see for yourself.

LODOVICO: I am sorry to find him like this.

[*Lodovico and Iago leave.*]

Scene 2 A room in Othello's house

[*Othello is talking to Emilia.*]

OTHELLO: You have seen her and Cassio together?

EMILIA: Yes, but they did nothing wrong. I heard every word they spoke.

OTHELLO: Did they never send you out of the room? To bring a drink, perhaps, or glasses, or her hat?

EMILIA: Never, my lord.

OTHELLO: That's strange.

EMILIA: My lord, on my life, I believe she is faithful. A devil has put these ideas into your head.

OTHELLO: Send her to me. Go! [*Emilia goes.*] Emilia is just a simple woman. A clever whore can hide all sorts of secrets.

[*Desdemona and Emilia come in.*]

DESDEMONA [*coldly*]: My lord, what do you want?

OTHELLO [*softly*]: Come here, my dearest. Look at me.

DESDEMONA [*frightened*]: What are you doing?

OTHELLO [*to Emilia*]: Go and shut the door. Call me if anyone comes. Go!

[*Emilia leaves them.*]

DESDEMONA [*falling to her knees*]: I am on my knees, Othello. I hear your angry words, but I do not understand them.

OTHELLO [*slowly*]: Who are you?

DESDEMONA: Your wife, my lord, your faithful wife.

OTHELLO: Yes, tell me your lies. Tell me you are honest!

DESDEMONA: God knows, I am.

OTHELLO: God knows, you are evil.

DESDEMONA: How, my lord? What have I done?

OTHELLO [*crying*]: Ah, Desdemona! Away, away, away!

DESDEMONA: Why are you crying, my lord? Are you angry with my father? Did *he* call you back to Venice? Is that what you believe? My lord, I lost my father when I married you.

OTHELLO: Oh God, make me sick, make me poor, destroy all my hopes – and I will be patient. But how can I live like this?

DESDEMONA [*crying*]: What have I done?

OTHELLO: What have you done? I cannot say the words. The smell of your crimes sickens God himself. Are you not a whore?

DESDEMONA [*crying*]: No. I am faithful to my husband.

OTHELLO: Then you must forgive me. I was mistaken. You look like Othello's wife – the whore from Venice. [*He calls Emilia.*] You, woman, come. [*Emilia comes in.*] Stay here with her and lock the door. [*He goes.*]

EMILIA: What's happening? How are you, my lady?

DESDEMONA [*pale and speaking slowly*]: I think I am dreaming.

EMILIA: What's the matter with my lord?

DESDEMONA: With who?

EMILIA: Your husband, my lady.

DESDEMONA: I have no husband. Do not talk to me now, Emilia. Tonight, put my wedding sheets on my bed. Now call your husband.

[*Emilia leaves, and returns with Iago.*]

IAGO: What do you want, my lady? How are you?

DESDEMONA: I cannot say. I have never suffered like this before.

IAGO: What's the matter, lady?

EMILIA [*very worried*]: Iago, my lord called her a whore. Now her heart is breaking.

IAGO: Why did he do that?

DESDEMONA [*crying*]: I do not know. It is not true.

IAGO: Don't cry, don't cry. How has this happened?

DESDEMONA: Only God knows.

EMILIA [*angrily*]: *I* know! An evil man, a dirty dog, has told Othello lies about my lady. That's what has happened!

IAGO: No, that's not possible.

DESDEMONA: If it is true, God forgive that man.

EMILIA: No, he should die and go to hell! She's done nothing wrong.

IAGO: Quiet, woman!

DESDEMONA: Oh, good Iago, go to Othello now. Tell him I will always love him dearly. I am not a whore. How I hate that word!

IAGO: Don't cry, my lady. I don't believe he is angry with you. Something is worrying him. Everything will soon be all right again.

[*Desdemona and Emilia leave. Iago goes out into the street and meets Roderigo.*]

IAGO: Hello, my friend. How are you?

RODERIGO [*coldly*]: Tired of listening to your lies, Iago. You've taken all my money, and I haven't even spoken to Desdemona.

IAGO: Roderigo, listen. [*He puts his hand on Roderigo's arm.*]

RODERIGO: I want my money back. If I don't get it, you will feel my sword.

IAGO [*warmly*]: Now you're speaking like a man! Give me your hand, friend. You've waited a long time for this, but now success is coming. Tonight, Roderigo, your luck will change.

RODERIGO: How? Tell me more.

IAGO: Listen. Othello is leaving Cyprus, and Cassio will take his place. But if Cassio dies, Othello will stay – and Desdemona, too. You must kill Cassio. I know where he's eating tonight – with his girl, Bianca. I'll be there to help you. Let's go, it's almost dinner-time. We have work to do!

[*They leave.*]

Scene 3 At the door of Othello's house

[*Lodovico and his servants are leaving Othello and Desdemona, after dinner with them. Emilia is with Desdemona.*]

LODOVICO: Good night, my lady, and thank you for this evening.

DESDEMONA: You are welcome, Signor.

OTHELLO: I will walk with you, Lodovico. Oh, Desdemona.

DESDEMONA: My lord?

OTHELLO: Go to bed. I will return soon. And tell Emilia to go.

[*Othello, Lodovico and servants leave. Desdemona and Emilia go inside, into the bedroom.*]

EMILIA: He looks calmer, my lady.

DESDEMONA: He told me to go to bed. And I must send you away. Good Emilia, give me my nightclothes and then leave. We must not make him angry again.

EMILIA [*angrily*]: I hope he never comes back!

DESDEMONA [*warmly*]: Don't say that. I love everything about him – good and bad. Here, help me undress. [*She sits on the bed.*]

EMILIA: I've put your wedding sheets on the bed.

DESDEMONA: Good. Emilia, if I die, cover me with one of those sheets.

EMILIA [*taking Desdemona's shoes and ring.*]: My lady, don't talk like that.

DESDEMONA: My mother had a servant girl called Barbary. She was in love, and her lover left her. She always sang the same old song – she died singing it. Tonight I cannot stop thinking about Barbary and her song.

EMILIA: Shall I go and get your nightdress?

DESDEMONA: No. Stay here. [*singing*]

Oh, down by the river a girl sat alone;

Her eyes were all water, her heart was all stone.

[*speaking*] Take my dress. [*Emilia takes it.*] Quickly. He'll soon be back. [*singing*]

Oh, cover me over with roses so sweet;

Put some at my head and put some at my feet.

[*speaking*] Can you hear him? He's at the door.

EMILIA: No, it's only the wind.

DESDEMONA [*singing*]:

The sun has gone in, and the moon's in the sky;
My lover has left me, and now I must die.
[*speaking*] Good night, Emilia. My eyes hurt. Does that mean I shall soon cry?

EMILIA [*very worried*]: I don't know, my lady.

DESDEMONA: Oh, Emilia! These men, these men! Tell me, are there really women who are unfaithful to their husbands?

EMILIA: There are, I'm sure. But I think bad husbands make bad wives. Our husbands run after other women, or get jealous, or hit us. Well, that's asking for trouble. We change – just like men.

DESDEMONA: Good night, good night. These times are sad.
But still I love what's good – and hate what's bad.

Act 5 Death

Scene 1 In the street at night

[*Roderigo and Iago are waiting for Cassio by a street corner.*]

IAGO: Here, hide in this dark corner. He'll come soon. Have your sword ready. Don't be afraid – I'm here.

RODERIGO [*nervously*]: Stay near. I may need you. [*to himself*] I have no great problem with Cassio. But Iago tells me I must kill him. So he will die.

IAGO [*to himself*]: It doesn't matter to me who kills who. No, Cassio must die. [*He looks around the corner.*] Here he comes.

[*Cassio arrives.*]

RODERIGO [*running forward*]: It's Cassio! Now, die! [*He attacks him with his sword.*]

CASSIO: My coat is thick and protects me. Let's see if yours is the same! [*He cuts Roderigo with his sword. Roderigo falls.*]

RODERIGO [*screaming*]: Oh, he's killed me!

[*Iago runs to them, wounds Cassio in his leg, and hides again.*]

CASSIO [*falling down*]: Oh, I am hurt. Help! Murder! Murder! [*Othello comes in.*] Help! Light! Someone get a doctor!

OTHELLO [*to himself*]: Excellent! Iago has killed Cassio. Your lover is dead, whore, and you will soon follow him.

[*Othello leaves, and Lodovico and Gratiano arrive.*]

CASSIO: Are there no guards? Lights! Murder! Murder!

GRATIANO: What's happening? Someone's hurt.

RODERIGO [*weakly*]: Oh, help!

LODOVICO: Two or three people are wounded.

[*Iago comes in with a light.*]

IAGO: Who's there? Who's hurt?

LODOVICO: We don't know. We can't see them.

CASSIO [*calling from the ground*]: Here, here! Help me!

IAGO: What's the matter?

GRATIANO [*to Lodovico*]: It's Othello's ensign. I know his voice.

RODERIGO [*calling from the ground*]: Oh, help me here!

IAGO [*seeing Roderigo*]: Ah! Here's the killer! [*He kills Roderigo with his sword.*] Help! Is anyone there? [*Lodovico and Gratiano come to him.*] Signor Lodovico, is it you? [*He sees Cassio.*] Here's poor Cassio, badly wounded.

GRATIANO: Cassio?

IAGO [*sounding very sad*]: Cassio, what have they done to you?

CASSIO [*weak and in pain*]: My leg is cut in two.

IAGO: God help us! Bring more light! [*taking off his shirt*] I'll tie my shirt around the wound. Bring a chair for him! Be calm, good Cassio, help is coming. Who is the dead man? [*He holds the light over Roderigo.*] Oh! My dear friend Roderigo!

GRATIANO: Roderigo, from Venice! I knew him well!

[*Some servants arrive with a chair.*]

IAGO: Oh, the chair, at last. [*He helps to lift Cassio.*] Carry him carefully. I'll get the General's doctor for him. Cassio, this man was my friend. Why were you fighting?

CASSIO: I don't know! I don't know the man! He suddenly attacked me!

IAGO [*to the servants*]: Be careful with him! [*The servants carry Cassio away.*]

[*Emilia arrives.*]

EMILIA [*worried*]: Oh, Iago, what's the matter?

IAGO: Roderigo and his friends have attacked Cassio in the dark. Roderigo is dead, and Cassio badly wounded. The others have escaped.

EMILIA: Oh, poor Cassio!

IAGO [*to Gratiano and Lodovico*]: Signors, let's go to Cassio. Emilia, go and tell my lord and my lady about this. [*to himself*] At last I see that everything is going well for me.

Scene 2 In the bedroom of Othello's house

[*Desdemona is asleep in bed. Othello comes in with a light and locks the door behind him.*]

OTHELLO: How pale and innocent she looks, lying here asleep. But she must die, or she will do more evil to men. Before I pick this lovely rose, I'll smell it one last time. [*He kisses her.*] Oh, she is so sweet! One more kiss, one more.

DESDEMONA [*waking up*]: Who's there? Othello?

OTHELLO [*quietly*]: Yes, Desdemona.

DESDEMONA: Come to bed, my lord.

OTHELLO: Are you ready to meet God, Desdemona? You must ask Him to forgive you before I kill you.

DESDEMONA [*sitting up, frightened*]: Are you talking of killing?

OTHELLO: Yes, I am.

DESDEMONA: Then God help me. I know I am innocent. But I am afraid of you. Will you kill me for loving you?

OTHELLO [*loudly*]: Quiet, woman!

DESDEMONA: Why are you shaking? Why are you angry?

OTHELLO: That handkerchief I gave you. You gave it to Cassio.

DESDEMONA: No, on my life! Send for him and ask him!

OTHELLO: Speak carefully and do not lie. You are on your deathbed.

DESDEMONA [*very frightened*]: Oh, God help me! I never loved Cassio, never gave him anything!

OTHELLO: I saw the handkerchief in his hand – saw it with my own eyes. Oh, your lies turn my heart to stone.

DESDEMONA: He found it then. I never gave it to him! Call him here! Ask him to explain!

OTHELLO: He has spoken. I know he has enjoyed your body.

DESDEMONA: No! It isn't true! He can't say that!

OTHELLO [*laughing*]: You're right! He cannot say anything. Honest Iago has silenced him for me.

DESDEMONA: Oh, I am full of fear! Is he dead?

OTHELLO: Yes, a thousand times dead.

DESDEMONA: Oh, there is some evil here, some terrible lie!

OTHELLO: What, are you crying for your lover?

DESDEMONA: Oh, my lord, I want to live! Do not kill me!

OTHELLO: No, you must die. [*He pushes her down on the bed, and holds his hand over her mouth.*]

EMILIA [*calling from outside the room*]: My lord, my lord!

OTHELLO: Who's there?

EMILIA: Oh my lord, I must speak to you.

OTHELLO [*to himself*]: It's Emilia – [*looking at Desdemona*] Ah, she's dead – She's bringing the news that Cassio is dead. No more movement? She's gone. If Emilia comes in, she'll speak to my wife. Wife? I have no wife. Oh, God, are the sun and moon still in the sky, and Desdemona gone?

EMILIA: Please, my lord, I must speak to you!

OTHELLO: Come in. [*He unlocks the door and Emilia comes in.*]

EMILIA: Oh my lord, there's been a terrible murder. Cassio has killed a young man called Roderigo.

OTHELLO: Roderigo dead? And is Cassio dead?

EMILIA: No.

OTHELLO: Cassio not dead? Then the wrong man has died!

DESDEMONA [*weakly*]: Oh murder, murder!

EMILIA: Oh God! That was my lady's voice! [*She runs to the bed, finds Desdemona, and tries to lift her.*] Help, oh help! Sweet Desdemona, talk to me!

DESDEMONA [*falling back on the bed*]: I am dying an innocent death.

EMILIA: Who has done this?

DESDEMONA [*very softly*]: Nobody. I myself. Goodbye, Emilia. Goodbye to my kind lord. [*She dies.*]

EMILIA [*screaming at Othello*]: You killed her. Oh, you are the blackest devil in hell!

OTHELLO [*shouting*]: She was a whore. Cassio had her. She was guilty. Ask your husband – he knew it all.

EMILIA [*very quietly*]: My husband?

OTHELLO: Yes. He told me. He is an honest man. He hates the evil these women do.

EMILIA [*crying*]: Oh, my poor lady! My husband told you she was unfaithful?

OTHELLO [*impatiently*]: Yes, yes, woman! My friend, your husband – honest, honest Iago!

EMILIA [*shouting*]: Oh, how could you believe him! He lied to you!

OTHELLO: Silence, woman!

EMILIA: Oh, you can't hurt me now. I'm not afraid of your sword! I'll tell the world! [*shouting*] Help, help! The Moor has killed my lady! Murder! Murder!

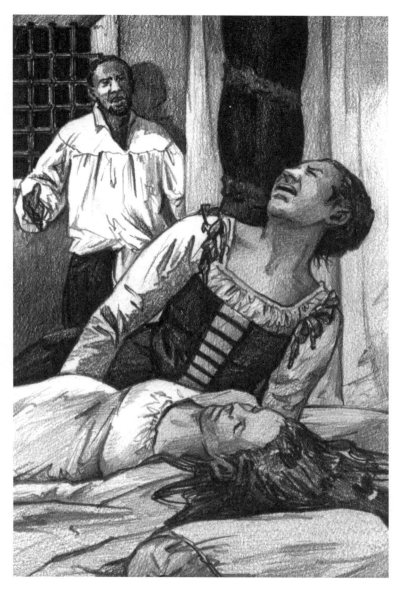

'You killed her.'

[*Montano, Gratiano and Iago come in.*]

MONTANO: What's the matter? What's happening, General?

EMILIA [*turning to Iago*]: Iago, what have you done? Did you tell my lord that my lady was unfaithful to him with Cassio?

IAGO: Yes. It's true. Be quiet, woman! [*He pushes her away.*]

EMILIA: No! You told a lie, a terrible, evil lie. I will not be quiet. Here she is, murdered in her bed. [*She points to the bed.*]

MONTANO AND GRATIANO: Oh, God help her!

OTHELLO [*calmly*]: It is true, sirs.

EMILIA: This is a terrible crime, and you are guilty, Iago.

IAGO: Are you out of your mind? Go away! Go home!

EMILIA: Sirs, I must speak. Perhaps I shall never go home again.

OTHELLO [*falling onto the bed and crying*]: Oh, oh, oh!

EMILIA: Yes, that's right, scream and cry! You have killed the sweetest, most innocent lady in the world.

OTHELLO: She was guilty! I killed her, but she was guilty!

GRATIANO: Poor Desdemona, I am glad your father's dead. Your marriage broke his heart. Thank God he cannot see this.

OTHELLO: Yes, she died a terrible death. But Iago knows what she did. She loved Cassio. She even gave him my gift to her, the handkerchief my mother gave me.

EMILIA [*putting her hands over her mouth*]: Oh my God!

IAGO [*holding her by her arms*]: Shut your mouth, woman!

EMILIA [*pushing him away*]: No! I will speak!

[*Iago takes out his sword*]

GRATIANO [*to Iago*]: Stop! Put down your sword!

EMILIA [*to Othello*]: You stupid, stupid man! I found your handkerchief and gave it to my husband. He often asked me to steal it.

IAGO [*screaming at Emilia*]: You're lying, whore!

EMILIA: I am not. [*to Othello*] Murderer! You have killed your wife for nothing.

OTHELLO [*to Iago*]: You must die for this.

[*Othello starts to take out his sword but Montano stops him. Iago runs at Emilia and wounds her with his sword, then runs out.*]

EMILIA [*weakly, falling by the bed*]: I will die by my lady's side.
MONTANO [*to Gratiano*]: Take the Moor's sword. Come, guard the door. I must stop Iago escaping.

[*Montano and Gratiano run out.*]

OTHELLO: I cannot live now. The end must come.
EMILIA: What were the words of your song, lady? Can you still hear me? I will die singing to you. [*singing softly*] Oh, cover me over with roses so sweet. [*speaking*] Moor, she was innocent. Moor, she loved you. [*She dies.*]
OTHELLO [*calling to Gratiano*]: Come in. I want to speak to you.

[*Gratiano comes in.*]

GRATIANO: What do you want to say?
OTHELLO: I have a good sword. Shall I fight you? For what? Do not fear me. This is the end of my journey. [*He goes to the bed, and looks at Desdemona.*] Oh, poor lady. Your face is as pale as the sheets you lie on. [*He takes her hand.*] Cold, cold, my girl, my innocent girl. Oh devils, burn me with all your fires! Throw me into the deepest hell, to suffer for ever! Oh, Desdemona, oh!

[*Lodovico and Montano come in. Servants carry in Cassio in a chair. Two soldiers bring Iago in.*]

LODOVICO [*looking around*]: Where is Othello?
OTHELLO: Here I am. I am the man who was Othello. [*He runs at Iago and wounds him with his sword.*]
LODOVICO [*to Montano*]: Take his sword.
IAGO: I'm wounded, but not killed.
OTHELLO: I am glad! I want you to live and suffer, not to die! For

me now, death means happiness.

LODOVICO: Iago has told us part of the story. Did you and he plan Cassio's death?

OTHELLO: Yes.

CASSIO: Dear General, I did nothing to hurt you.

OTHELLO: I believe it now, and ask you to forgive me. Will you ask this devil, Iago, why he did it?

IAGO: Ask me nothing. I will never speak again.

GRATIANO: You will speak. Pain will open your mouth.

LODOVICO [to Othello]: You do not yet understand everything. We have found letters in Roderigo's pockets. One of them shows he meant to kill Cassio. And here's one he wrote to Iago.

OTHELLO: That devil! But Cassio, how did you get the handkerchief I gave to my wife?

CASSIO: I found it in my bedroom. Iago says he put it there.

OTHELLO: Oh, how could I believe him!

CASSIO: And Iago used that poor silly young man, Roderigo. Roderigo attacked me when I was drunk. Iago told him to do it.

LODOVICO: Othello, you must go with us. Cassio is now the general here. And we will throw Iago into prison. Come!

OTHELLO: Wait. A word or two before you go. I have been a faithful soldier for Venice. Well, all that is finished now. Do not try to excuse what I did. I killed my love, and now I must die. [He takes out a knife and wounds himself in the chest.]
[to Desdemona]
I kissed before I killed you. Now see this.
Killing myself, I die with one last kiss.
[He falls onto the bed next to her and dies.]

LODOVICO [to Iago]: Look, you dog, at what you have done. Here, on this bed, lie the people you have destroyed. Cassio, you must punish this devil from hell. He must suffer, as these poor people suffered.
I will now sail to Venice, for my part –
To tell the story with a heavy heart.

ACTIVITIES

Act 1

Before you read

1 *Othello* is a famous play by William Shakespeare. Work with another student and discuss these questions.
  a Do you know the names of any other plays by Shakespeare? Make a list.
  b Which of the plays on your list have you seen in a theatre or as a film (in any language)?
  c Talk about one of these plays. Is it happy or sad? Did you enjoy it? Describe some of the people in the play, and what happens to them.
  d Compare your list with the lists of other students. Which plays do most people know? Which play is the most popular with your class?

2 Look at the Word List at the back of the book. Which words are:
  a for people's jobs, or the positions that they have?
  b for parts of a play?
  c about fighting?
  d about good and bad?

3 Read the Introduction to the play and answer these questions.
  a How is Othello helping the Duke and people of Venice?
  b In what way is Othello different from most people in Venice?
  c What is the feeling that destroys Othello?
  d Circle the words that describe Othello when the play begins.
    brave   cold   successful   happy   lonely
  e When was *Othello* written?
  f 1) Where was Shakespeare living when he wrote the play?
    2) How was he earning money?
  g Who plays Othello in the 1952 film of the story?

4 Act 1 is called 'Love and War'. Othello is a general and he must go to war. What will happen to the woman he loves? How will she feel? What do you think?

49

While you read

5   Are these sentences true (✔) or untrue (✗)?

   a Iago is happy to be Othello's ensign.   .....

   b Roderigo wanted to marry Desdemona.   .....

   c Brabantio knows where his daughter is.   .....

   d Othello wants to fight Brabantio.   .....

   e The Turks are attacking Venice.   .....

   f Othello has married Desdemona.   .....

   g Othello and Desdemona often met at Brabantio's house.   .....

   h Desdemona wants to go to Cyprus with Othello.   .....

   i Othello asks Iago to look after his wife.   .....

   j Iago wants to get his hands on Roderigo's money.   .....

After you read

6   Correct these sentences.

   a Brabantio calls Othello a murderer.

   b Brabantio says that his daughter could never love an old man.

   c Desdemona loved listening to Othello's songs.

   d The Duke tells Brabantio not to be friendly with Othello.

   e The Duke tells Othello to sail to war the next day.

   f Iago tells Roderigo to follow his heart.

7   Describe these people's feelings for the other person. Give reasons for your opinions.

   a Othello and Iago

   b Iago and Roderigo

   c Brabantio and Othello

   d Cassio and Iago

   e Brabantio and Desdemona

8   Discuss these questions. Give reasons for your opinions.

   a Is Desdemona right to marry Othello in secret? Is her father right to be angry?

   b How can parents make sure that their children don't marry secretly?

Act 2

Before you read

9 Discuss these questions with another student. What do you think?

    a What will Iago do to make trouble for Cassio?

    b What will he plan to do to Othello?

    c How will he use Roderigo in his plans?

While you read

10 Put these sentences in the correct order, 1–9.

    a Cassio and Roderigo fight, and Cassio hits Roderigo.   .....

    b Iago and Desdemona arrive in Cyprus.   .....

    c Cassio wounds Montano with his sword.   .....

    d Iago tells Cassio to ask for Desdemona's help.   .....

    e Iago makes Cassio drunk.   .....

    f Othello arrives in Cyprus and meets Desdemona there.   .....

    g Cassio arrives in Cyprus.   .....

    h Othello is angry with Cassio and punishes him.   .....

    i Iago tells Roderigo that he must start a fight with Cassio.   .....

After you read

11 Discuss these questions with another student. What do you think?

    a What mistakes does Cassio make?

    b Do Iago and Emilia have a good marriage?

    c Does Cassio really love Desdemona?

    d How does Desdemona feel about Cassio?

12 Work with another student. Have this conversation. One of you is a friend of Montano's. He is badly wounded after the fight, and you are visiting him.

    Student A: You are Montano's friend. Ask what has happened to him.

    Student B: You are Montano. Answer your friend's questions.

Act 3

Before you read

13 Which of these will happen? What do you think?

   a   Cassio will ask Desdemona to speak to Othello for him.

   b   Emilia will help Iago with his evil plan.

   c   Othello will begin to get angry with Desdemona.

   d   Iago will tell Othello not to be a jealous husband.

   e   Othello will believe that Desdemona is unfaithful to him.

   f   Othello will continue to believe that Iago is his friend and an honest man.

While you read

14 Who says these words? Who or what are they talking about?

   a   'I never knew a better, more honest man.'

   .... / ....

   b   'He will send me away. Then he will forget me.'

   .... / ....

   c   'Please call him to you and forgive him.'

   .... / ....

   d   'If my love for you ever dies, my life will be at an end.'

   .... / ....

   e   'That is a sickness that eats men's hearts.'

   .... / ....

   f   'Do other men enjoy what belongs to me?'

   .... / ....

   g   'She dropped it by accident, and I picked it up.'

   .... / ....

   h   'He was only dreaming.'

   .... / ....

   i   'I gave him no reason to be jealous.'

   .... / ....

   j   'What's this, Cassio? A gift from a new friend?'

   .... / ....

After you read

15 Put these words in the right places in the sentences below. Use
each word only once.

from   with   to   of   about   for   at   on   in

a Emilia is sorry to hear ..... Cassio's problem.

b Cassio often went ..... Othello to Desdemona's house.

c Othello begins to feel a pain ..... his heart.

d Desdemona tells Othello that his guests are waiting ..... him.

e Desdemona's first gift ..... Othello was a handkerchief.

f Othello thinks Desdemona is unfaithful ..... him.

g Iago once stayed the night ..... Cassio's house.

h Othello says his heart is now full ..... hate.

i Cassio meets Bianca ..... the way to her house.

16 Discuss these questions with another student. What do you think?

a Who is (or are) suffering from jealousy? Why are they jealous
and who are they jealous of?

b Who is (or are) feeling sad? Why?

c Who is (or are) telling lies?

Act 4

Before you read

17 Discuss these questions with another student. Give reasons for
your answers.

a How will Iago use Cassio and Bianca in his plan to destroy
Othello?

b Will Desdemona understand why Othello is changing?

c Will either Roderigo or Emilia start to understand Iago's plans?

While you read

18 Circle the correct words.

a Othello cannot stop thinking about *a letter / a handkerchief*.

b Othello says that he feels a pain in *his heart / his head*.

c Iago talks to Cassio about *Desdemona / Bianca*.

d Bianca is *happy / angry* when she sees Cassio.

e Othello tells Iago that he *will speak / will not speak* to his wife before her death.

f *Brabantio / The Duke* calls Othello back to Venice.

g When Othello hits Desdemona, Lodovico is very *surprised / frightened.*

h Emilia *believes / doesn't believe* that Desdemona is faithful.

i Desdemona says she *will always love / has stopped loving* Othello.

j Othello tells Desdemona to *wait for him with Emilia / go to bed alone.*

After you read

19 Put these words into the right sentences.

gives   sings   follows   hits   shakes   cries   laughs   asks

a When Othello is sick he falls down and ..... .

b Bianca loves Cassio, but he ..... at her.

c Bianca ..... Cassio everywhere.

d Lodovico ..... Othello a letter from Venice.

e Othello calls his wife a devil and ..... her.

f When Othello attacks Desdemona, she ..... .

g Roderigo ..... Iago to give him his money back.

h Desdemona ..... as she gets ready for bed.

20 Discuss these questions.

a Which of these people understands most about what is really happening?

Emilia   Lodovico   Desdemona

b What does each of them think is happening?

Act 5

Before you read

21 Work with another student. Discuss these questions. What do you think?

a What can Desdemona do to save herself? Is there anything that she can say? Is a happy end to the story still possible for her?

b Which of these people will still be alive at the end of the play?

Othello   Cassio   Emilia   Iago   Desdemona
Roderigo

While you read

22 Who

a	attacks Cassio first?	....
b	wounds Roderigo?	....
c	wounds Cassio?	....
d	kills Roderigo?	....
e	gets help for Cassio?	....
f	tells Desdemona that Cassio is dead?	....
g	kills Desdemona?	....
h	tells Othello that Cassio is alive?	....
i	tells Othello that Iago lied to him?	....
j	kills Emilia?	....
k	wounds Iago?	....
l	kills Othello?	....

After you read

23 Are these sentences right or wrong? Correct the ones that are wrong.

a Cassio is saved from a sword wound by his thick coat.
b Desdemona is killed in her own bed.
c Othello hits Desdemona before he kills her.
d Othello kills Desdemona with his sword.
e Desdemona is able to speak to Emilia before she dies.
f Emilia is afraid that Othello will kill her, too.
g Othello believes that Iago has killed Cassio.
h Iago agrees to talk about his crimes.

24 Work with another student. Discuss these questions.

a What should happen to Iago now?
b How does Cassio feel? What does he know about Othello and Iago now? Will he make any changes to his life in future?
c Why did Othello believe Iago? Why didn't he believe Desdemona?

d What is your opinion of Othello? Do you feel sorry for him?

e Was Emilia guilty in any way, or is she completely innocent?

Writing

25 Write a letter from Othello to Desdemona, asking her to marry him in secret. Then write her reply.

26 Compare Desdemona and Emilia. In what ways were the two women different? Which did you like best?

27 After Othello's death, write about him for a newspaper. Give the news of how he died. Tell the story of his life.

28 Write a letter from a worried Lodovico to his relatives in Venice after he has seen Othello hit Desdemona.

29 In your opinion, who is the most interesting person in this play? Explain why.

30 Lodovico has to take the news of Othello's death to the Duke of Venice. Write the speech that he will make.

31 Write a modern short story about jealousy for a student magazine. Your story can be sad or funny.

32 Imagine that you are going to make a film of this play. Which actors will you choose? Will you leave the story in Shakespeare's time or change it to the present day? Will you change the story in any way?

33 Write the story of Desdemona's death for a popular newspaper. Call it 'The Handkerchief Murder'.

34 Cassio has now taken Othello's place as general. Write the speech that he makes to his soldiers.

Answers for the activities in the book are available from the Penguin Readers website. A free Activity Worksheet is also available from the website. Activity Worksheets are part of the Penguin Teacher Support Programme, which also includes Progress Tests and Graded Reader Guidelines. For more information, please visit: www.penguinreaders.com.